50

American Serial Killers You've Probably Never Heard Of

Volume Nine

Robert Keller

**Please Leave Your Review of This Book At
http://bit.ly/kellerbooks**

ISBN: 9798642872499

Table of Contents

Robert Alston

Between 1991 and 1994, the city of Greensboro, North Carolina, was plagued by a series of gruesome murders of young women. The victims were snatched from the street and driven to isolated locations where they were raped, strangled and, in some cases, dismembered. Body parts were then scattered, with little attempt at concealment, to be found by horrified passersby.

The first murder occurred in April 1991 when 23-year-old JoAnne Robinson's naked body was found discarded on a sidewalk. An autopsy would show that she'd been raped and then throttled to death. Six months later, a utility crew was working in a wooded area near Jackson Middle School when they discovered the severed head and arm of 26-year-old Sharon Martin, who'd been reported missing weeks earlier.

At this point, the police did not connect the two homicides. But that would change seven months later with the discovery of yet another mutilated corpse. Nineteen-year-old Shameca Warren's naked and decapitated body was discovered in a vacant lot, close to the site where JoAnne Robinson had earlier been found. It suggested to police that a serial killer might be at work in the area, but no sooner had they begun working on that theory than the killer dropped out of sight. He'd remain under the radar and apparently inactive until December 1993, when he re-emerged to snuff out the life of 41-year-old Lois Williams. This latest victim's strangled corpse was found inside Piedmont Memorial Cemetery, although investigators did not at this point link it to the other homicides due to the lack of postmortem mutilations.

However, the police would not be left guessing for long. In January 1994, a woman stumbled into a Greensboro police station and reported that she had been kidnapped, raped and strangled, then left for dead under a bridge on Youngs Mill Road. According to the victim, she'd been walking along Martin Street in southeast Greensboro when a man in a dark blue car stopped and offered her a ride home. Instead, he drove her to Dudley High School where he raped and beat her, then choked her until she passed out. She'd woken under the bridge with such severe bruising to her throat that she'd been barely able to breathe. After clawing her way up the bank, she'd managed to flag down a passing motorist who brought her to the hospital.

To detectives listening to this story, the attack bore remarkable similarities to the series of murders they were currently investigating, the victim kidnapped, raped and strangled. In this case, however, the killer had slipped up in leaving his victim alive. Now she was shown a photo array of known sex offenders, and she unerringly pointed to one, the dreadlocked figure of 29-year-old Robert Sylvester Alston.

Arrested within a week, Alston would prove to be an unrepentant killer. After striking a deal to avoid the death penalty, he readily admitted to four murders, earning himself a sentence of life in prison without parole. But it was Alston's attitude at trial that marked him out for the cold-hearted killer he is. The former dishwasher spent much of his time on the stand, taunting the grieving relatives of his victims, grinning broadly as he refused to reveal what he'd done with their body parts. "Only me and God will have those answers," he smirked as he was led away to begin his life behind bars. Robert Alston remains a suspect in two similar murders committed in Greensboro during the same time period.

Clinton Bankston

For pure ferocity, there are few crimes that can match those committed by Clinton Bankston. Just 16 years old on the night of August 15, 1987, Bankston entered a house in the Carr's Hill suburb of Athens, Georgia, and proceeded to hack the residents to death with an axe. Ann Morris, 63, her 59-year-old sister Sally Nicholson, and Sally's daughter, 22-year-old Helen, were so badly mutilated that they would later have to be identified from dental charts. The juvenile killer then ransacked the house before fleeing in his victims' car. It was that vehicle, carelessly parked outside the home of his half-brother, Curtis Johnson, that would lead to his arrest the following day.

Once in custody, Bankston made no pretense at innocence. Indeed, he not only boasted about the murders but added two more to his tally. He admitted to killing university professors Glenn and Rachel Sutton during an invasion of their Oglethorpe Avenue home in April 1987. On that occasion, police had responded to a call from concerned neighbors who were worried about the lack of activity at the house and the drapes that had still not been drawn by mid-afternoon. Officers had entered to find the couple knifed to death, their bodies rolled up in a carpet, and blood pooled on the floor and spattered on the walls and furnishings.

Yet, despite the brutality of those killings, they were not marked by the extreme overkill of Bankston's Carr's Hill massacre. The killer had a ready explanation for that. He said that he had an accomplice named Chris Ward and that it was he who called the shots. It was Chris who had committed the murders and Chris who had sexually assaulted two of the victims. According to Bankston, he had managed to curb some of Chris's maniacal tendencies during the Sutton killings. But Chris was getting stronger. If the police didn't catch him soon, he would undoubtedly kill again.

This defense was an interesting take on an excuse often proffered by captured serial killers. These killers frequently blame their crimes on an alternate personality. Ted Bundy called his "the entity" while Hillside Strangler, Kenneth Bianchi, gave his alter-ego the name "Steve Walker," and William Heirens dubbed his "George Murman." In Bankston's case, he insisted that "Chris" was not a dissociative personality but a real person, and a dangerous one at that.

The police, of course, did not believe him. Nonetheless, they were compelled to launch a search for Chris Ward, a search which, as expected, came up empty. Bankston's family had certainly never met Ward or even heard of him. They insisted, though, that Ward must be real since there was no way that Clinton could have committed these atrocities. The boy had a good heart, they said. He wouldn't hurt a fly. His main interest in life was the pop star, Michael Jackson. People often told Bankston that he resembled

Jackson, and he encouraged the comparison by dressing like the famous musician.

But Bankston had a far more nefarious claim to fame than that of a Michael Jackson impersonator. He was a stone cold killer and now he'd have to face the consequences of his actions. Despite an attempt by his defense counsel to declare him not guilty by reason of insanity, Bankston was convicted on five counts of first-degree murder.

On May 12, 1988, (his seventeenth birthday) Bankston was sentenced to five terms of life imprisonment. The D.A. later confirmed that he would have sought the death penalty but for Bankston's age at the time of the murders. State law prohibited the execution of persons who had committed their crimes while under the age of 16 years. Clinton Bankston had escaped the needle by just a few months.

Richard Beasley

On the evening of November 9, 2011, a man named Jeff Schockling answered a knock at the door of his farmhouse and found a stranger on his porch, bleeding profusely. "Call 911," the man gasped, "I've been shot." Schockling immediately complied.

That call brought Noble County Sheriff Stephen Hannum racing to the remote Ohio farm, where he found the stranger sitting at a picnic table, clutching his wounded arm. The man identified himself as Scott Davis and then told the sheriff a bizarre story. He said that he'd come to Ohio to take up a job as a farm manager, which he'd secured after answering an ad on Craigslist. He'd initially met his potential employer, "Jack," at the Shoney's Restaurant in Marietta. He'd then left his truck and trailer in the restaurant parking lot and had driven with Jack to the farm he was to manage. They had been accompanied by a teenage boy.

Along a desolate stretch of road, Jack had suddenly stopped the car and asked Davis to help him retrieve some tools that he'd left in the brush. Instead, Jack had led him into the trees, drawn a gun and shot him. Had the weapon not jammed after that first shot, Davis believed that he would surely have been killed. He'd escaped by running into the woods and had eventually reached the Schockling farmhouse. As for motive, Davis believed that he'd been lured there to be robbed and killed. Perhaps that was why Jack had asked him to bring along all his belongings, including his Harley Davidson motorcycle.

Initially, the sheriff was skeptical of Davis's story. But having established that Davis's belongings (including his Harley) were indeed sitting in a trailer in Marietta, an investigation was launched. Over the following days, detectives tracked the IP address used to place the Craigslist ad to an address in Akron. The owner of the house denied placing the ad but suggested that it might have been placed by Ralph Geiger, a former tenant. He also said that Geiger had left his cellphone number with him.

On November 16, the police got the landlord to call Geiger and to keep him on the line long enough to run a trace. Geiger was taken into custody by a SWAT team while he was still on the phone. His accomplice, 16-year-old Brogan Rafferty, was arrested soon after and revealed his friend's true identity. "Geiger" was actually Richard Beasley, an ex-con with a long arrest record for burglary, firearms offences, and running a prostitution ring. He was currently a fugitive from justice, wanted on a parole violation in Texas.

One week after his arrest, Brogan Rafferty struck a deal with prosecutors that allowed him to plead to reduced charges in exchange for his testimony against Beasley. Although Rafferty would later renege on the deal, all of the interviews he gave were recorded, and the recordings would later be played in court. They told a grim tale.

According to Rafferty, Beasley's first victim was a man named Ralph Geiger, who he'd lured from a homeless shelter in early August 2011. The motive for this murder wasn't financial but to steal Geiger's identity, since Beasley was currently wanted by the police. Beasley had then launched his Craigslist scam. First he'd snared a man named David Pauley, who had been shot to death and buried in the woods; then he'd lured Scott Davis, who had escaped.

There was also a fourth victim. After the failed attempt on Scott Davis's life, Beasley had attracted a new mark, a man named Timothy Kern. Kern had arrived on Sunday, November 13, driving a rusty old sedan with an ancient TV set on the back seat beside a few garbage bags filled with his clothes. This was a disappointment to Beasley since the purpose of his scam was to rob his victims of their possessions. Aggrieved by Kern's lack of material wealth, Beasley shot him anyway, out of spite. Kern was buried in a shallow grave behind an abandoned mall in western Akron. Four days after that murder, Richard Beasley would be in police custody.

Richard Beasley went on trial in April 2013 and was convicted on three counts of first-degree murder and sentenced to death. Brogan Rafferty, having reneged on his plea bargain, was sentenced to life in prison without parole.

Howard Belcher

During October 2002, police in Atlanta, Georgia, were called to four very similar crime scenes. In each instance, the victims were gay men who had been bludgeoned and strangled to death in their own homes. Robbery was an obvious motive since cash and valuables had been taken. At two of the scenes, the killer had also left a gas oven on, probably with the intention of causing an explosion that would destroy evidence. There was also another clue linking the murders; at least two of the victims frequented a gay bar called Bulldogs in downtown Atlanta. The venue was particularly popular with African-American men.

The first to die was 27-year-old Leroy Tyler, who was found inside his Clarkston apartment on October 5, 2002. That same day, police were called to the scene of another murder, this one in Midtown. The victim was 40-year-old Mark Schaller, a wealthy gay man and frequent patron of Bulldogs. Officers entered his gas-filled Monroe Drive condo to find Schaller with his hands bound tightly behind his back with a necktie. He'd been beaten to death.

Five days later and another gay man was found murdered. Matthew Abney was 45 years old and worked as an assistant manager at Wal-Mart. The condition of his corpse was remarkably similar to that of Mark Schaller. Abney had been tied up and his partially nude body showed signs of a beating, although death was determined to be by strangulation. As with the Schaller murder, the place had been ransacked and the gas oven had been left on. That detail was a red flag to Atlanta PD. It appeared that they were dealing with a serial killer, one whose preferred victims were gay men.

And the killer was far from done. On October 28, 35-year-old Artilles McKinney was found dead in his home in Duluth, Georgia. The conditions of this murder were so similar to the others that there could be little doubt that the same killer was responsible. McKinney was gay, he was a patron of Bulldogs, and he'd been tied up and strangled to death. He'd also been robbed of valuables, including his 1994 Lexus.

An APB was immediately issued on the missing vehicle, and it paid dividends two days later when a young African-American man was pulled over while driving the car in College Park. Taken in for questioning, the man identified himself as Howard Milton Belcher, aged 26. He readily admitted that he was a male prostitute and confessed that he often picked up "tricks" at Bulldogs. However, he denied knowing any of the murdered men or having anything to do with their deaths.

That was never going to fly, of course, since Belcher had been arrested while driving one of the victims' cars. No doubt realizing how that must look, Belcher changed his story. He now admitted that he'd met McKinney at Bulldogs and had gone home with him. However, he insisted that there had been a third man in the house, and it was this man who'd killed McKinney. Then he changed his story again, saying that McKinney had died of a heart attack while they were having sex. Unfortunately for Belcher, this version of events was contradicted by the autopsy report.

In the end, Howard Belcher eventually broke down and admitted to killing Artilles McKinney after the victim picked him up at Bulldogs and propositioned him for sex. Belcher would ultimately face trial separately for the four murders, receiving a life sentence in each case. That, according to Belcher, was a disappointment. He'd hoped to be sentenced to death. "I wanted the death penalty," he informed the court. "I really didn't want anyone to represent me."

FOOTNOTE: Since his imprisonment, Howard Belcher has revealed that he is HIV-positive. He remains the main suspect in several other murders of gay men in the Atlanta area.

Arthur Bomar

Aimee Willard was a young woman with a bright future. The 22-year-old was a star lacrosse player at George Mason University in Fairfax, Virginia; she had just been named in the All-Conference Team in both soccer and lacrosse; she had dreams of coaching high school sports after graduation. But on the night of June 20, 1996, all of those dreams were extinguished.

Aimee was on her way home to Brookhaven, Pennsylvania, after enjoying drinks with friends at a local bar, Smokey Joe's Tavern. Somewhere along the road, she encountered a predator. Her car was found the next morning on the Springfield exit from I-476, still running and with the driver's door open. That sparked a massive search for the missing co-ed, one that would be resolved tragically within 24 hours. Aimee's body was found some 17 miles away in a trash-strewn lot in North Philadelphia. She had been beaten to death with a tire iron, the blows delivered with such force that her skull was shattered. The postmortem would also reveal that she'd been viciously raped.

The murder of Aimee Willard, a police captain's daughter, sparked
a massive investigation but one that was hampered from the start.
The police had plenty of evidence, including DNA, tire tracks, and a
unique burn mark on the victim's back. The problem was that they
lacked a suspect to match it to. Despite the best efforts of
investigators, the trail soon went cold.

Nearly two years later, on May 29, 1998, a young woman was
driving along I-95 late at night when she was rear ended. The
driver of the other vehicle tried to get her to stop, but the woman
refused. Looking in her rear-view mirror, she memorized the
license plate number of the vehicle that had hit her. Then she put
her foot down and drove to the nearest police station, where she
reported the incident. That decisive action undoubtedly saved her
life. When police ran the plate, it showed that the car was
registered to Maria Cabuenos, a 25-year-old lab technician who
had been reported missing in March that year.

The incident on I-95 left investigators to wonder whether this was
somehow linked to Aimee Willard's murder. Was this how her
killer had forced her to stop? By rear ending her vehicle?
Unfortunately, it was not a theory they were able to test, since they
had no idea who had been driving the stolen vehicle. That is, until
June 5, 1998, when a man named Arthur Bomar was arrested on a
parole violation.

Bomar was a convicted murderer. Back in 1978, he'd shot a man to
death in Nevada in a dispute over a parking space. Just 19 at the
time, he'd been sentenced to five years to life and had been
paroled in 1990 after serving eleven years. Thereafter, he'd been

allowed to return to his hometown of Philadelphia. Nevada's problem was now Pennsylvania's.

Over the next seven years, Bomar was in and out of prison on charges ranging from assault to burglary to car theft. Recently, he'd stopped keeping his parole appointments, and that was why he now found himself in custody. At the time of his arrest, he was driving Maria Cabuenos's car, the same vehicle that he'd used to ram his intended victim on I-95.

Bomar readily admitted that he'd stolen the car, but he denied having anything to do with the disappearance of Maria Cabuenos or with Aimee Willard's murder. However, the evidence against him soon began to stack up. Inside the car was blood belonging to the missing woman. Then police tracked down Bomar's own vehicle, a 1993 Ford Escort that he'd recently sold to a scrap yard. It provided several links to the Willard murder, including hair and fibers and a match to the tire marks found at the crime scene. Investigators also now understood where the burn on Aimee's back had come from. It matched the oil pan of the Escort. It appeared that the terrified woman had burned herself while trying to crawl under the vehicle to escape her attacker.

There was other evidence, too. Bomar had admitted to a former girlfriend that he'd murdered Aimee Willard. He'd told her that he'd followed Aimee from Smokey Joe's Tavern and had pulled her over by flashing a fake police badge. The girlfriend was more than happy to share that information with police. The most damning evidence, though, was a DNA match which linked Bomar to the semen recovered from Aimee Willard.

This was about as comprehensive a case as any prosecutor could hope to bring into a courtroom. And yet Arthur Bomar insisted on maintaining his innocence and claiming that he was a victim of racism. That stance did not help him at trial. Convicted of capital murder, he was sentenced to death. He currently awaits execution. Bomar has never been charged with the murder of Maria Cabuenos even though her skeletal remains were recovered shortly after he was convicted. Who knows how many other young women have died at his hands.

Eugene Britt

It is not often that you hear of a serial killer trawling for victims on a ten-speed bicycle. But Eugene Britt wasn't your average psycho killer. He rode that same bicycle fifteen miles along the Interstate to work every morning, oblivious to the horns and curses of drivers; he never had a bank account nor a telephone number in his life, and he never got past the fourth grade in school. In fact, Britt sometimes appeared oblivious to the world around him. With an IQ of just 60, he was well below the generally accepted mark for mental impairment.

But for all of that, Britt did possess a certain level of smarts, the kind of smarts that a predator needs for stalking prey. Like most serial killers, he preyed on the weak and vulnerable – children, prostitutes, and down-and-outs. Britt chose his victims wisely, targeting those whose disappearances would not cause too much of a stir. It was only when he changed his M.O. and abducted a little girl that the police eventually closed in on him.

The case that would lead to Eugene Britt's downfall was the murder of 8-year-old Sarah Paulsen. Sarah went missing from a neighborhood in Portage, Indiana, on August 22, 1995, sparking a massive search that would be tragically resolved that same day with the discovery of her raped and brutalized body. That, in turn, led to one of the biggest homicide inquiries conducted in the area in years, an investigation that was presented with a tantalizing clue on its very first day. Several witnesses reported seeing a black man cycling aimlessly around the area on a blue bicycle at the time the little girl disappeared.

Was this perhaps the abductor? Detectives worked the lead relentlessly, but it wasn't until November 1995 that it broke for them. Then, the manager of a local diner called the police and suggested that the man they were looking for might be one of his former employees, Eugene Britt. According to the tipster, he'd fired Britt on August 22, the same day that Sarah was abducted. Britt had left in the early afternoon, cycling away on his blue 10-speed. That would have given him plenty of time to reach the neighborhood from which the little girl had been snatched. The reason for Britt's dismissal? Sexual harassment of a female co-worker.

It sounded like a promising lead, and detectives therefore tracked down the suspect and brought him in for questioning. It appeared, however, that Britt's cycling days were over. He was now confined to a wheelchair, the result of throwing himself in front of a train in a suicide attempt. He was also in confessional mood. The investigators had barely asked for his name when he said that he wanted to confess, not just to killing Sarah Paulsen, but to "others." He then began rattling off a litany of death.

Britt's killing spree had started in May 1995 when he dragged 40-year-old Deborah McHenry into an overgrown lot and throttled her into submission before raping her. He'd warned her not to look at him, but McHenry had looked and had recognized him. He and Deborah had been childhood neighbors and had played together as kids. Since she could identify him, he had strangled her.

About a month later, on June 24, Britt had snatched 13-year-old Nekita Moore from a street in Gary, Indiana, dragged her into an abandoned house and raped her. The child had begged for her life, telling Britt that she was only thirteen. Britt had strangled her anyway.

On August 13, Britt had followed his familiar M.O. to rape and murder Michelle Burns, strangling her because "she looked at my face when I told her not to." Two weeks later, he'd murdered Sarah Paulsen. "I was angry that day," he said, as though that justified the rape and murder of an eight-year-old.

Britt had claimed three more victims, even while the police were hunting him for the Paulsen murder. On September 2, he'd pulled Betty Askew into an abandoned house and ended her life, afterwards stealing $300 from her purse. Days later, he'd lured Tonya Dunlap into some woods with the promise of marijuana and then raped and killed her. Finally, he'd murdered 41-year-old Maxine Walker. The last two victims had yet to be discovered but Britt led officers to their decomposing bodies, left in woodland on the outskirts of Gary, Indiana.

Eugene Britt was eventually put on trial in 2006, eleven years after his deadly spree. There were strident calls in the community for his execution. Given his mental incapacity, that was never likely to happen. He was sentenced instead to consecutive life terms plus 100 years, meaning that he will never be released.

Thomas Bunday

The state of Alaska, with its vast wilderness and remote towns, provides the perfect hunting ground for a serial killer. And the state has produced its fair share of monsters, most notably Robert Hansen and Israel Keyes. Hansen, a keen hunter, took the idea of hunting humans quite literally. He would kidnap prostitutes in Anchorage, fly them out into the wilderness in a light aircraft, then give them a head start and begin stalking them with a high-powered rifle. As many as 21 women would meet this dreadful fate at his hands. Israel Keyes, possibly America's most meticulous killer, used Alaska as a base for his murderous sojourns around the country. It was only when he decided to commit a murder closer to home that he was eventually caught. By then, at least eight had been slain.

Thomas Richard Bunday is not as well-known as the aforementioned psychopaths. Indeed, there is very little information on the Air Force sergeant turned serial killer. This is probably because Bunday killed himself before he was charged with murder. Here's what we do know.

Between 1979 and 1981, five young women and an 11-year-old girl disappeared from the area of Fairbanks, Alaska. Initially, the police treated these as missing persons' cases. They believed that the women had simply left the area or, in the case of the pre-teen girl, run away from home. But when a thorough investigation turned up no trace of the missing, investigators began to suspect something more sinister.

And then the bodies started turning up, four of them found scattered along a 25-mile stretch of the Richardson Highway between Fairbanks and Eielson, a fifth in Hurricane Gulch, 150 miles to the south. Glinda Sondemann, 19, Marlene Peters, 20, Wendy Wilson, 16, Lori King, 19, and Cassandra Goodwin had all been shot in the head, and ballistics linked the first four to the same murder weapon. The youngest victim, 11-year-old Doris Oehring, was never found, but the police now knew that they had a serial killer stalking their streets.

Fairbanks is a city of around 31,000 residents, with a rate of violent crime that exceeds the US national average. Still, murder is quite rare and serial murder unheard of. The local authorities therefore called in the Alaskan State Police and a task team was established. Soon a hotline was in place and the leads were pouring in. It seemed that everyone in town had a neighbor or acquaintance who they thought might be a potential mass murderer.

In order to narrow their options, the task force contacted the FBI's Behavioral Science Unit and requested a profile of the killer. Unlike in the movies, however, these profiles can be a bit hit-or-miss. In the case of the Fairbanks killer, it was the latter. Rather than leading the police to their suspect, it was deflecting attention away from him.

Thomas Bunday, then serving as a technical specialist at the Eielson Air Force Base, was on the list because his car had been spotted in an area from which some of the victims had vanished. But he was just one of hundreds of suspects, and because he did not match the profile, he was initially ignored. It was only when that profile was revised, early in 1983, that the clues started slotting together, elevating Bunday to the top of the list. Detectives then went to question him, only to learn that he'd been transferred to Sheppard Air Force Base in Wichita Falls, Texas, two months earlier.

In March 1983, Alaska State Troopers Jim McCann and Chris Stockard departed for Texas to question Bunday. Armed with a search warrant, they arrived at his house in Burkburnett on Sunday, March 13. Executing their warrant, they soon found items linking Bunday to the murders in Alaska. (The exact nature of the items was never revealed, but given what we know about serial killers, they were probably mementos taken from his victims). Bunday, in any case, wasn't denying murder. He sat the detectives down and casually informed them that he was the killer they were looking for. The only murder he denied was that of Cassandra Goodwin which had always been in doubt anyway, due to the lack of a ballistic match.

It was a stunning admission but one that the Alaskan officers could not act on since they were out of their jurisdiction and did not have an arrest warrant. They therefore departed and immediately got to work obtaining the necessary paperwork. At around 2:00 p.m. on Tuesday, March 13, they were back, warrant in hand, ready to make an arrest. But they'd missed their suspect by minutes. Bunday's wife informed them that he'd just roared off on his motorcycle.

Bunday headed north, racing along US 183 as a light rain began to fall. Two miles south of the Red River bridge, he spotted a dump truck coming in the other direction. Opening the throttle on his Yamaha, he waited until the last moment and then veered the motorcycle directly into the path of the truck. He was killed on impact.

Frank Canonico

Of all the motives offered for serial murder, the one given by Frank Canonico must rank among the most bizarre. Canonico claimed that he killed his victims because he objected to them treating him as a sex object.

A native of Brooklyn, New York, Frank Canonico started his criminal career early in life. His specialty was stealing cars, and he was good at it. Unfortunately, he wasn't quite as proficient at the other side of the equation, getting rid of the merchandise. It resulted in successive arrests related to transporting vehicles across state lines. That, in turn, saw him spend time in a number of federal prisons. It was following his release from one such institution, in 1979, that he decided to hit the road, to see a bit of America. Over the next two years, he'd travel coast to coast, killing as he went. By some estimates, he may have claimed as many as 25 victims.

Canonico was a smooth-talker, not particularly good-looking, but handsome enough to attract the attention of female patrons at the sort of establishments he frequented. These were generally singles bars, where the idea was to meet someone, spend a pleasant evening in their company, and then to move on. And herein, lay Frank's problem. He wasn't looking for a good time, he was looking for true love. He was looking for the kind of woman who would turn down his advances on the first date and tell him to wait until they were better acquainted. Unfortunately, to quote the lyrics of Johnny Lee's hit country song, he was "looking for love in all the wrong places." And that angered him.

The murder that would ultimately lead to Frank Canonico's downfall occurred in Fort Lauderdale, Florida, in July 1981. Police had been called to the residence of a wealthy 60-year-old widow named Willine Wall. Questioning neighbors, they learned that Mrs. Wall had been seen over the previous two days in the company of a younger man. The man was described as "flashy," with an Afro hairstyle, a mustache and a somewhat flamboyant dress sense which included several thick, gold chains strung around his neck. According to witnesses, he drove a 1971 Lincoln Mark V.

The police reckoned that a man like that should be easy to find, and they were right. Within a day, the suspect showed up at a pawnshop where he tried to sell some of Willine Wall's valuables. The owner stalled him until the police arrived.

Once in custody, Canonico wasted no time in confessing to the murder. In fact, he told detectives about another woman he'd shot just a few days earlier in nearby Lauderhill. Forty-three-year-old Phyllis Schwartz had not yet been reported missing when police found her dead body in her apartment, exactly as Canonico had said they would. And the killer wasn't stopping there. He now claimed that he had killed "between 10 and 25" women on his travels around the country, committing murders in Louisiana, Nebraska, Tennessee, Arizona and California, as well as in Florida.

Investigators were initially skeptical about these claims, but many of the details that Canonico provided checked out. One case that police were particularly interested in was the slaying of Wanda

Brown, a 46-year-old German immigrant. Her body had been found with no identification in San Francisco's Hyde Park on May 25 and had been recorded as a Jane Doe. Now Canonico was able to clear up the details for them. He said that he'd met Ms. Brown in a bar, gone with her for a walk and shot her dead when she suggested some open air sex.

But Frank Canonico would never be tried for the Brown murder, or for any of the others he confessed to outside of Florida. He was indicted only of the killings of Willine Wall and Phyllis Schwartz. Convictions in those cases were enough to earn him consecutive life terms. As for Canonico's motive, it is easy to be skeptical. The more likely reason he killed the women was to rob them.

Daniel Corwin

It should have been clear to anyone who knew Daniel Corwin that he would come to a bad end. Obsessed with sex from an early age, Corwin committed his first rape when he was just fourteen years old. The victim was a 13-year-old girl who was babysitting at a neighbor's house. Unfortunately, she never reported the assault, leaving Corwin at liberty to attack other women.

As a high school senior in Temple, Texas, Corwin abducted and raped a female classmate and then stabbed her in the chest and left her for dead. The blade, however, missed the girl's heart, and she survived to name Corwin as her attacker. He was later convicted of aggravated rape and sentenced to 40 years in prison.

Corwin was paroled after serving just nine years of that sentence. And his time behind bars had done nothing to still his carnal impulses. In November 1987, he abducted a Texas A&M University student, drove her to a remote location and tied her to a tree. He then spent hours raping the unfortunate woman before slashing her throat and leaving her for dead.

Miraculously, Corwin had missed all of the major veins and arteries, and the woman was eventually able to free herself and crawl to the roadside. There, she was spotted and rescued by a passing motorist. Corwin, who had left his fingerprints on his victim's car, was arrested soon after. He made no attempt to deny the charge and was later convicted of attempted murder and sentenced to 99 years in prison.

But the attack on the co-ed was not Dan Corwin's only offense. It was only once he was behind bars that the full extent of his evil deeds would come to light.

During the nine months between Corbin's release and his arrest for the attack on the Texas A&M student, there had been a spate of savage murders in Huntsville, Texas. In February of 1987, 72-year-old Alice Martin was walking along a country road in Madison County when a man stopped beside her and forced her into his truck. He then drove the elderly woman to a remote area of Robertson County, where he raped her repeatedly before stabbing her four times in the back and then strangling her to death with a ligature.

Five months later, in July of 1987, a young woman named Debra Ewing was abducted from the parking lot of the Huntsville Vision Center, where she worked. Her brutalized corpse was later found in a remote area of Montgomery County. She'd been raped and her attacker had then strangled her to death with a ligature. She had also been stabbed twice in the chest.

Then, on Halloween evening in October 1987, a 36-year-old woman named Mary Risinger was washing her vehicle at a Huntsville carwash when a man approached, brandished a knife and tried to force her into his truck. Risinger, who had her three-year-old daughter in the car, put up a fierce struggle, but her bravery had a deadly consequence. She was fatally stabbed in the neck, the knife severing every major vein and artery. She bled to death on the cold concrete, while her frantic little girl watched from the car.

At the time of Daniel Corwin's imprisonment, all of these murders were still unsolved. And they would likely have remained so had Corwin not decided to confess them to a prison sociologist two years later.

At trial, Corwin's defense tried to plead insanity. Evidence was offered that Corwin had suffered two serious childhood head injuries that might have resulted in brain damage. Corwin himself testified that he periodically suffered from "tunnel vision" which could only be relieved through acts of violence. That, however, was not enough to sway the jury. They took just 25 minutes to find him guilty and to recommend that he be put to death.

Daniel Corwin was executed by lethal injection on December 7, 1998. He offered a long, rambling final statement during which he urged the state of Texas to reconsider the death penalty. He was pronounced dead seven minutes after the lethal cocktail of drugs began to flow.

Frederick Cox

Frederick Cox was 43 years old but looked older since a back injury had forced him to walk bent over with a cane. He was a ham radio enthusiast whose modest house in the Pine Hills suburb of Orlando, Florida, bristled with antennae. He shared that house with his common-law wife, two sons and two German Shepherd dogs. Neighbors didn't know a lot about him since he and his family kept mostly to themselves. He did, however, enjoy talking to young people in the neighborhood. Normally, he warned them about the dangers of drugs.

Then, on a humid afternoon in May 1997, Cox's somewhat secretive life would be exposed, not just to his neighbors but to the world. That was the day that the air resonated with the sound of sirens and a convoy of police vehicles screeched to a halt outside the Cox residence. Then, to the astonishment of onlookers, their grandfatherly neighbor was brought out in handcuffs, loaded into a cruiser and whisked away. What, they wondered, could old Mr. Cox possibly have done to warrant such attention? Quite a lot as it turned out.

Frederick Cox was born in Tallahassee, Florida, but spent most of his life in Orlando, save for a three-year stint in the Army in the early 1970s. He never married although, at the time of his arrest, he'd been in a long-term relationship with Rosena Murphy and had two sons with her. He had also, until his back injury, served one weekend a month with the U.S. Army Reserve. During his working career, he'd held down several jobs, including as an

Orange County correctional officer. Most recently, he'd been working as a telemarketer. So far, so mundane.

But scratch below the surface of Frederick Cox's oh-so-ordinary life and a different picture emerges. In 1988, he'd been arrested for indecent exposure after he was seen masturbating inside an adult book store. That matter had still not come before the courts when Cox was in trouble again. This time, he was caught in possession of marijuana.

Booked on drugs charges, Cox pleaded no contest and agreed to perform community service. He also volunteered for Mothers Against Crack Cocaine and was a tireless campaigner for that cause, drawing praise from the group's director. That was in 1991. Six years later and Cox apparently still saw himself as a different kind of community activist. He decided that he wanted to clear the streets of prostitutes.

At around midnight on March 12, 1997, 34-year-old Tracey Adams was driving along Pappy Kennedy Street in Orlando when she got a flat. She'd just got out to inspect the tire when a man pulled up in a tan Buick Park Avenue and propositioned her for sex. Adams angrily informed the man that she wasn't a prostitute. He responded by drawing a gun and pulling the trigger, hitting Tracey in the arm before speeding off.

Tracey Adams was seriously injured, but she was lucky. She had survived. Two weeks later, in March 1997, the naked body of 40-

year-old Patricia Logan was found beside a wooded trail off Colonial Drive. Logan was known to police as a sex worker. She had been shot in the head and her corpse posed in what detectives described as "a degrading position."

Over the next month, two more women – 22-year-old Mary Ann Voepel and 28-year-old Stephanie Singleton – would fall prey to the same killer. But their bodies would lie undiscovered until April 29, and by then there had been yet another attack.

Yolanda Neals was a veteran of the streets. She knew how to take care of herself, and she had an eye for danger. On April 16, Neals was standing on the corner of Church and Tampa when a man approached in a tan Buick and offered her $25 for sex. He looked, according to Neals's later statement, "real nice, professional-like." And so she accompanied him to a secluded lot near Universal Studios and got out of the car when he asked her to. Then, suddenly, he drew a gun and started firing.

Neals was hit in the cheek, the bullet plowing its way through flesh and exiting her neck. But then her survival instinct kicked in, and she was fleeing into the night, even as the bullets flew around her. But for her swift action, she would certainly have been killed. Her testimony would later play a big part in Frederick Cox's conviction.

But it was a chance encounter with his other surviving victim that led to Cox's arrest. In May 1997, Tracey Adams was shopping at a grocery store when she spotted the man who had shot her two months earlier. With admirable calm, she followed him out of the store and jotted down his license plate number which she passed on to police. Cox was arrested soon after.

At trial, the forensic case against Frederick Cox was overwhelming, with ballistics linking his licensed firearm to the shootings and blood from at least one victim found in his car. Many expected him to get the death penalty. Instead, he was spared the needle and sentenced to life without parole.

John Crutchley

John Crutchley was a lonely kid, a science geek with an interest in technology which he transformed into a healthy income during his high school years. Crutchley's side gig at that time was repairing electronic equipment. Later, he obtained a physics degree from Defiance College and a Master's in engineering from George Washington University. That earned him a well-paid position with Delco Electronics Corporation in Kokomo, Indiana, although he eventually left under a cloud over missing equipment. By the mid-70s, he was living in Fairfax, Virginia, and working for Logicon Process Systems. It was during this time that teenaged girls and young women began to go missing from the area.

The first missing woman to be linked to John Crutchley was his girlfriend, 25-year-old Debbora Fitzjohn. Debbie inexplicably vanished in 1977, shortly after she'd been seen visiting Crutchley at his trailer. He was questioned, of course, but denied having anything to do with her disappearance. He was still sticking to that story when the young woman's skeletal remains were found by a hunter in October 1978. With no evidence to connect Crutchley to the crime, the police were forced to let the matter drop.

But Debbora Fitzjohn was not the only woman to disappear from Fairfax during the time that Crutchley lived there. Neither was Fairfax the only town to experience a spate of vanishings while Crutchley was around. There was a rash of disappearances from a Pennsylvania neighborhood that he lived in; there was the disappearance of the teenaged Lyon sisters from Wheaton, Maryland; there was the vanishing of Kathy Lynn Beatty from Aspen Hill, Maryland. Some of these women later turned up dead while others were never found. In all of these cases, the common denominator was John Crutchley.

And yet, while police might have suspected Crutchley of being a serial killer, there was never any evidence to pin the murders on him. It wasn't until Crutchley moved to Florida in the early 1980s that his true character was revealed to the world.

In late November 1985, a driver traveling along a road near Malabar, Florida, was astonished to see a teenaged girl, naked and cuffed at the wrists and ankles, crawling along the roadside. The driver stopped and helped the girl into his car, then drove home and called the police and an ambulance.

The teenager was rushed to hospital where doctors were astonished to find that, although she had no major injuries, she had lost over 40 percent of her blood. Later, she'd be able to resolve that mystery for detectives. She said that she'd been hitchhiking and had been picked up by a man who had driven to a residence in Malabar, saying he had to make a stop there. He'd then pounced on his passenger, strangling her into unconsciousness. She woke to find herself naked and strapped to a kitchen table, a video camera hovering over her. Her abductor then raped her while videotaping the action.

Then, the rapist did something truly bizarre. He inserted a needle into the girl's arm and began tapping her blood into a glass. This he drank, savoring it like it was a fine wine. He explained to his victim that he was a vampire and would "feed off her" for several days. Over the next 12 hours, he raped the girl twice more, each time drawing and drinking blood. He would likely have continued until she died of blood loss but the following morning, he left the house briefly, allowing the girl to escape. Asked if she would be able to lead officers back to the house where she'd been attacked, the girl answered with an emphatic yes. The property turned out to belong to John Brennan Crutchley.

Crutchley was arrested and would subsequently plead guilty to rape and kidnapping and accept a 25-year jail term. But it was items found hidden in his house that caught the attention of investigators – a stack of stolen but expired credit cards, several items of female jewelry, and a collection of index cards, on which Crutchley had recorded details of the sexual performance of various unnamed women.

Were these the trophies of a serial killer? Robert Ressler, the famed FBI profiler, certainly thought so, especially when he started looking into Crutchley's background and discovered at least ten cases of women who had mysteriously vanished while

Crutchley was in the vicinity. One of those, of course, was Crutchley's former girlfriend, Debbora Fitzjohn.

Unfortunately, there was no physical evidence linking Crutchley to the missing women. He hadn't been charged back then and he wasn't now. Instead, he served his time as a model prisoner and was released in 1996, having spent just eleven years behind bars.

However, Crutchley's freedom would be of short duration. Just a day after his release, he was arrested for violating his parole after he tested positive for marijuana. A conviction for that offense meant that the "three strikes law" was now in effect. That meant that Crutchley was going back to prison for life.

On March 30, 2002, John Crutchley was found dead in his cell, with a plastic bag pulled over his head. Initially, it was thought that he'd committed suicide, but the Florida Department of Corrections later announced that he'd died while practicing autoerotic asphyxiation.

Charles Davis Jr.

Charles William Davis Jr. is one of the more unusual serial killers you are likely to encounter. The son of a police lieutenant, Charlie might well have followed in his father's footsteps. Instead he embarked on an equally admirable career path. He decided to become an ambulance driver.

Yet, despite the apparently altruistic nature of Davis's career choice, there were other aspects of his behavior that were not so commendable. Women considered him creepy, and a number of his female co-workers had lodged complaints about his overt sexual advances. In an era when such harassment was not taken as seriously as it is today, he escaped on each occasion with a warning. Sexual harassment was, in any case, the least of Charles Davis's crimes.

On New Year's Eve 1975, a young woman named Kathleen Cook attended a party at a night club situated inside a Baltimore shopping mall. Kathleen was with her husband that night, and the two of them met other relatives at the club. During the evening, she spoke briefly with a young man who told her that he was a detective with the Baltimore Police Department. A short time later, there was an announcement over the P.A. about a car that was blocking an entrance. Kathleen heard her license plate number read out and told her husband that she was going out to move the car.

Once outside, Kathleen encountered the young detective again, although now he was far less friendly than he'd been earlier. Drawing a gun, he bundled Kathleen into her car and instructed her to drive to a secluded spot behind the mall. There he punched her in the face, forced her to perform oral sex, and then savagely raped her. Finally, he pumped four .38 caliber bullets into her body. Then he stepped calmly from the car, walked back to his own vehicle, and drove away.

Charles Davis had been at the nightclub that night, and some witnesses thought that they'd seen him talking to the victim. Brought in for questioning, Charlie wasn't confirming or denying it. "There were so many pretty women there that night," he smirked. "And I talked with a lot of them." With no reason to suspect otherwise, the cops let him go. He'd later hint darkly to his work colleagues that he knew a lot more than he'd told the police and that his "connections on the force" had got him out of a bind.

Nearly eight months later, on August 24, 1976, the body of another young woman was found in remarkably similar circumstances. Peggy Pumpian was found inside her vehicle which had been abandoned on the I-95, just south of Baltimore. She had been shot several times, and an autopsy would reveal that she had been beaten and raped. A ballistics match would link this murder to that of Kathleen Cook.

Ten months went by with no sign of resolution in either the Cook or Pumpian murders. Then, on July 20, 1977, a couple of state troopers spotted a VW Beetle driving erratically on the outskirts of Baltimore. They followed at a distance while running the plates and soon learned that the registration number did not match the vehicle. They then pulled the driver over and recognized him as Charles Davis.

One of the troopers asked Davis if he could search the vehicle, which Davis agreed to. Soon the officer was pulling a brand new CB radio out from under the seat. When the officers called in the serial number to check if it was stolen, they learned that it was not but that it had been purchased with a stolen credit card. The card belonged to a woman named Carol Willingham and had been taken from her during the course of a rape/robbery on February 23. Charles Davis was then arrested and taken into custody. Carol Willingham would later pick him out of a lineup as the man who had assaulted her. Davis, however, was not about to wait around for his day in court. Out on bail, he fled to Reno, Nevada, remaining there for two months before he was tracked down and extradited to Maryland.

At this stage, Davis was looking at a long prison term for rape and robbery. But he was about to drop a bombshell. Back on home turf, he informed his jailors that he had something "big" to tell them. Thus it was that, on September 4, a properly Mirandized Charles Davis confessed to the murders of Kathleen Cook and Peggy Pumpian.

Davis would later be convicted of both murders and sentenced to life in prison without parole. But what makes this case truly remarkable is not the murders Davis confessed to, but the ones he didn't. He remains a strong suspect in three more homicides. In each of these cases, an anonymous caller alerted the authorities, and an ambulance was dispatched to the scene. The driver in each case was none other than Charles Davis. It is speculated that he deliberately dumped the bodies along the route he was working. It seems that the retrieval of the bodies somehow enhanced his enjoyment of his horrific deeds.

James Duquette

In the early hours of April 4, 1980, 18-year-old waitress Anne Marie Preimesberger had just finished a long shift at a diner in Mequon, Wisconsin. She was exhausted and eager to get home, so when a couple of male customers offered her a lift, she readily accepted. Mequon was a small, quiet town. What was the worst that could happen?

But before the car had even pulled out of its slot, Anne Marie had cause to regret her rash acceptance of the ride. Another man slid into the vehicle, this one burly and smelling of sweat. He slid into the backseat with her. Before Anne Marie even had a chance to speak out, to say that she'd changed her mind, the car started moving. Uncomfortable, fearful of the situation she'd gotten herself into, Anne Marie said a silent prayer that it would all be alright. It was a prayer that would go unanswered. Anne Marie Preimesberger's body was found the next day, discarded under a highway overpass ninety miles away near Grand Chute, Wisconsin. An autopsy would show that she had been raped by multiple assailants before being beaten and strangled to death.

The investigation into Anne Marie Preimesberger's death was a difficult one for the small Mequon force. With no eyewitnesses and scant physical evidence, it appeared that the killer (or killers) might get away with murder. But the investigators never gave up, and eleven years later, they finally had their man. By then, James Duquette Jr. was serving a life term in Massachusetts for the kidnapping and rape of a 13-year-old girl in Southampton. He had also been convicted of another murder in Wisconsin.

The battered, nude body of 14-year-old Tara Kassens had been found in a field outside Mequon on July 4, 1987. Tara's parents had reported her missing the previous day, after she disappeared while riding her bicycle. Duquette, who had been visiting his former in-laws in Ozaukee County at the time, soon emerged as a suspect. He would ultimately be convicted, and it was then that police began to wonder about his possible involvement in the death of Anne Marie Preimesberger.

It was Duquette's two cohorts who would fill in the details of the Preimesberger murder. Jeffrey Whitman and Lou Dahlman had been the other two men in the car that night. Both took the deal offered by prosecutors in exchange for their testimony, accepting prison terms of 20 years and 15 years respectively for their roles in the young woman's death. According to Whitman, it was Duquette who'd called the shots, Duquette who had beaten and strangled Anne Marie, Duquette who had instructed him and Dahlman to rape the terrified young woman. At one point during the ordeal, Anne Marie had looked at him beseechingly and whispered, "Help me." Whitman, terrified of Duquette, had told her, "I'm sorry. I can't."

The murders of Anne Marie Preimesberger and Tara Kassens and the rape of the Southampton teen are not the only violent sex crimes of which James Duquette is guilty. We can say this with confidence because a predator like Duquette will never stop attacking women while he is at liberty to do so. Duquette has been implicated in several other homicides and strongly linked to the murder of 24-year-old Denise Laack, whose battered corpse was found in a wooded area near Henry, Illinois, on November 18, 1979. At the time of her murder, Denise was living in Appleton, Wisconsin, James Duquette's home town.

Danny Figueroa

If Danny Figueroa had a hero, it was probably John Rambo, the fictional survivalist/war hero played by Sylvester Stallone in the series of 1980s blockbusters. Figueroa liked to dress like Rambo, in military fatigues, headbands and face paint; he liked to get out in the desert around his home in Perris, California, and stalk small game; he liked to pretend that he was on some high-stakes secret mission. He even liked to hang out with local teens and teach them survival skills and bushcraft. To them it was a game. To Danny Figueroa, it was serious. Soon, it would turn deadly serious.

On the afternoon of May 13, 1986, 53-year-old Reynold Johnson was standing in his yard in Aguanga, California, when he was struck in the chest by a bullet fired from a high-powered rifle. Johnson was dead even before he hit the ground, and neighbors later reported a man dressed in military fatigues fleeing the scene. However, the subsequent investigation turned up no clues, no motive, and not a single suspect.

Two weeks later, in nearby Riverside County, 19-year-old Ray Webber was driving a pickup on his brother's ranch when he was struck by a sniper's bullet. He was found slumped over the steering wheel of the truck, his skull shattered by a single bullet. Again, the police were perplexed. The victim had not been robbed, his truck had not been taken, and he had no enemies that anyone knew of. There appeared to be no motive for his murder.

Five days passed. On June 15, an illegal alien was crossing a field in Imperial County when he was approached by a man in uniform. Taking the uniformed man for a Border Patrol officer, the illegal meekly surrendered, whereupon the "officer" raised his weapon and fired. Left for dead, the severely wounded man crawled to the road where a passing motorist stopped and drove him to a hospital in El Centro. Later that day, the man was able to give police a description of his assailant, and a search was launched. It was during that search that a patrol picked up Danny Figueroa, in full Rambo garb, stalking the brush.

Figueroa was taken in for questioning and emphatically denied the shooting. He claimed that he was a survivalist, out scouting for places to hole up in the event of an apocalypse. Looking back into Figueroa's past, investigators found that he had a record of minor offences dating back to his teens. They were certain that his victim would pick him out of a lineup. However, when the injured man was shown a photo array that included Figueroa, he demurred and said he wasn't sure. With no evidence to hold Figueroa, the police were forced to let him go. That would have tragic consequences for two more innocent people.

On June 8, Robert Jimenez was barbequing in his back yard in Indio, California, when he was struck by three bullets. Jimenez wasn't killed outright, but as he started crawling towards the safety of his house, the killer broke cover, ran towards him and pumped another round into the back of his head. By the time his family found him, just minutes later, the shooter was long gone.

By now, police in Southern California knew that they had a serial sniper on their hands, someone who was certain to kill again unless they stopped him. Unfortunately, they were not able to do so before he claimed another victim. On June 17, 72-year-old Mary Langerich took her dog for a walk in Redlands, California, and never returned. A search was launched and turned up her body three hours later, shot to death beside a gravel path. This time, at least, the police had a clue. A man dressed in paramilitary garb had been spotted in the area, a man whose description closely matched the "survivalist" officers had questioned in El Centro.

On June 21, detectives showed up at Danny Figueroa's home to question him. Danny's family said that he was out "camping" and told the officers that they would have a hard time finding him since he knew the surrounding desert like "his own back yard." That would turn out to be no idle boast. Despite a massive manhunt involving roadblocks, tracking dogs, and helicopters sporting the latest in infrared technology, Figueroa remained at large for over a week, until his luck eventually ran out and he was captured in Reche Canyon.

Danny Figueroa went on trial in San Jacinto, California, during June 1987. Convicted on three counts of murder, he was sentenced to 66 years to life.

Wayne Adam Ford

On the evening of November 3, 1998, a man walked into a Sheriff's station in Humboldt County, northern California, pulled a Ziploc bag from his coat pocket and placed it on the counter. It appeared to contain a chunk of raw meat which, on closer inspection, turned out to be the severed breast of a woman. The man was then hustled into an interview room where he identified himself as Wayne Adam Ford, a 36-year-old long-haul trucker. With tears running down his cheeks, he told detectives that he had done some "very bad things." Then he launched into a confession during which he admitted to four murders.

Three of the victims, according to Ford, were prostitutes he'd picked up at truck stops along his route over the last two years. The other was a woman he'd abducted from a parking lot in Fontana, California.

The first to die was a Jane Doe, strangled, stabbed, and then dismembered inside Ford's trailer in October 1997, her remains dumped in a channel near Eureka, California. This unfortunate woman had been so thoroughly mutilated that the police were never able to determine her identity. She had been sliced down the middle and almost disemboweled; her head and hands had been hacked off and so had her breasts. All in all, seven body parts were recovered, including the torso, which was found in marshland, and an arm that washed up on a beach. Some of the remaining body parts would be found packed inside a freezer in Ford's trailer, near Arcata, California. According to later laboratory analysis, Ford had tried to cook some of the flesh.

Ford's other victims could, at least, be named. The body of 26-year-old Tina Renee Gibbs, a Las Vegas prostitute, had been found in a Kern County aqueduct on June 2, 1998. She had been strangled. Ford said that he'd picked Gibbs up in Vegas and they'd had sex in a motel there. She'd later accompanied him on the drive to California and he'd murdered her in his truck.

Four months later, the nude body of 25-year-old Lanett White was pulled from a San Joaquin County irrigation canal. White had last been seen on September 20, when she'd rushed out to a grocery store to buy milk for her baby. She'd never returned.

The final victim was 29-year-old Patricia Ann Tamez, found floating in the California Aqueduct in San Bernardino County in October 1998. Tamez was a college graduate from an upper middle-class family but had fallen into prostitution due to her drug habit. She too had been strangled and one of her breasts had been hacked off. This was the piece of flesh that Ford had carried into the sheriff's station in Humboldt County.

According to Ford, he hadn't wanted to hurt his victims. He'd merely been deflecting the rage that he felt towards his ex-wife over her refusal to allow him to see his son. And his reason for surrendering was equally astounding. Ford said that he could feel his anger growing towards his ex and knew that he would eventually kill her. He had handed himself over because he did not want his son to end up an orphan.

Wayne Adam Ford was arraigned for four counts of first-degree murder on November 6, 1998. However, the trial would remain bogged down by legal motions and interdicts for an incredible eight years before it eventually came before the courts. When it did, Ford was found guilty on all four counts. He had privately told family members that he deserved to die for what he'd done and hoped for the death penalty. The jury didn't disappoint on that score. Ford currently resides on San Quentin's death row, awaiting his date with the executioner. He remains one of the very few serial killers who has willingly surrendered to the authorities.

Warren Forrest

The 1970s were a dangerous time for a young woman to be hitchhiking around Washington State. This was a time when one of America's most feared serial killers, Ted Bundy, prowled the streets looking for victims. Bundy usually sought his prey on college campuses, but he was known to pick up hitchhikers, with devastating results for any woman who accepted a ride from him. But Bundy wasn't the only misogynistic psychopath trawling the Evergreen State during that decade. Another was a man named Warren Forrest who, although not as prolific as Bundy, was every bit as depraved.

On February 11, 1972, an 18-year-old Clark College student named Barbara Ann Derry set off from Vancouver, Washington, hoping to hitch a ride to Wildwood. She promptly disappeared and remained missing until March 29, when her naked body was found at the bottom of the silo at the Grist Mill, a county park. She had been killed by a single knife wound to the heart, inflicted by a narrow blade.

Barbara Ann Derry's murder would remain unsolved for the next two years. Then, on July 11, 1974, another young hitchhiker went missing. Krista Kay Blake, age 19, was last seen getting into a blue van driven by a white male. She was later found buried in a shallow grave at Tukes Mountain, with her hands and feet hogtied behind her with baling twine.

Just a week later, on July 17, a man driving a similar blue van picked up a 15-year-old hitchhiker on State Highway 502, near Ridgefield, Washington. Once the girl was inside the vehicle, the man threatened her with a knife, then drove her to the Tukes Mountain area where he forced her from the vehicle and tied her to a tree. This location was just 100 feet from where Krista Blake had been found.

With the terrified girl apparently secured, her abductor left, although he said that he'd return soon. Knowing that she'd likely die if she did not get free, the desperate girl chewed through her bonds and escaped. She then hid in a nearby field, remaining there until daybreak when she was found by a Parks employee. When police arrived to search the area, they found that the man had returned during the night and had removed all incriminating evidence.

On October 1, 1974, another young woman was abducted by a man in a blue van, driven into the mountains and raped. She was then strangled unconscious and stabbed five times in the chest before her body was hidden behind a log and covered with brush. Her attacker then departed, apparently believing that she was dead. Amazingly, she was not. The victim later regained consciousness and staggered to a road, where she was helped by a passing motorist.

Less than two weeks later, Clark County deputies were investigating this latest abduction when they uncovered the bodies of two young women, buried close together in shallow graves. One of the victims was identified as 18-year-old Carol Valenzuela and was later confirmed to be a victim of Ted Bundy. The other was never identified but is believed to have been killed by the man in the blue van, Warren Forrest. He would claim a sixth victim before he was eventually caught. Gloria Nadine Knutson was last seen in downtown Vancouver on May 31, 1974, and discovered near Lacamas Lake nearly four years later. A seventh victim, 16-year-old Jamie Grissim, has also been strongly linked to Forrest.

But linking a suspect to a victim and proving that he is guilty in a court of law are two entirely different things. Warren Leslie Forrest was not your typical psycho killer. He was a married man and the father of two children; he was a military vet who had served in Vietnam. On the other hand, he owned a blue 1973 Ford van like that driven by the killer; he had once worked for the Clark County Parks and Recreation Department and knew the area where the bodies were found; he had been off work on the days of each of the abductions; and a gun, duct tape and baling twine similar to that used on the victims had been found in his van. The surviving victims also picked him out of a lineup.

In the end, the decision was made to charge Forrest with only one murder, that of Krista Blake. Items belonging to Blake had been found in Forrest's home. At trial, Forrest was found guilty of first-degree murder and sentenced to life in prison. He has been eligible for parole since 2014. All applications for early release have thus far been turned down.

Wayne Garrison

When Wayne Garrison was a little boy, he broke the neck of a pet rabbit that he had begged his grandmother to buy for him. That earned him a sound beating, but it did not dissuade him from other acts of cruelty against animals. He once decapitated a neighbor's dog and was fond of impaling his grandmother's chickens with a sharpened stick.

Such acts of wanton cruelty are regrettably fairly common among fledgling serial killers. In fact, these juvenile psychopaths will usually escalate their violent acts against animals before eventually graduating to humans. Usually, that transition occurs in their early twenties. In the case of Wayne Garrison, it happened far sooner.

Garrison was just 13 years old when he murdered his 4-year-old cousin Dana Dean on October 31, 1972. The little girl had been playing with Garrison at her home in Tulsa, Oklahoma, when he wrapped a strip of cloth around her neck and began twisting it, increasing the pressure until she started turning blue, maintaining it until she stopped breathing. He then dragged the body under the crawlspace of the house where it was later found by Dana's father. Questioned by police, Garrison initially denied that he'd killed his cousin, then admitted it but insisted that it had been an accident. The abrasions and bite marks on the child's corpse said different but, as a juvenile, Garrison was never going to face the full might of the law. A juvenile court ordered that he be committed to a state hospital. He was still an inmate there when he killed again.

In May 1974, while Garrison was on a pass from the hospital, a 3-year-old neighbor, Craig Neal, went missing. Garrison, then 14, was questioned by police during the course of their investigation and admitted that he had played a game of hide and seek with Craig. He denied that he knew the boy's whereabouts.

That was a lie, of course. Craig's strangled body was found stuffed in a garbage bag and hidden in the crawlspace beneath the Garrison residence. His penis had also been cut off. Backed into a corner, Wayne eventually admitted that he'd suffocated the little boy although, as before, he insisted that it had been an accident. The outcome this time was a second-degree manslaughter conviction and four years in a juvenile prison.

At just 14 years of age, Wayne Garrison was already a multiple child murderer. And he would not even serve the ridiculously lenient sentence he'd been given. In March 1977, having spent just two years at the Oklahoma State Reformatory, Garrison was released back into the community. He was now 17 years of age and supposedly rehabilitated. The children of Tulsa were in grave danger.

And yet, apparently, Wayne Garrison was able to keep his murderous instincts at bay for over a decade. During that time, he married, fathered a son, started a business, divorced. Then, on June 20, 1989, there was a familiar scenario involving Garrison when a 13-year-old boy named Justin Wiles disappeared. Justin had last been seen hanging around Garrison's business, Chopper's Body Shop. When his dismembered body was found at Bixhoma Lake four days later, Garrison was immediately a suspect.

Despite their suspicions, the Tulsa police lacked the evidence to bring charges against Garrison. And just months after the murder, their suspect sold up and quit town, moving to Charlotte, North Carolina. He was soon back in Oklahoma, though, when he was charged for filing a false insurance claim in the state during October 1989. That earned him an 18-month prison stint, which he completed in June 1991. He then moved back to North Carolina.

On February 9, 1996, Garrison was arrested for abducting and drugging an 11-year-old boy, an offense that would see him sentenced to five years behind bars. By now, Justin Wiles had been dead for nearly seven years, but the Tulsa police had never given up hope of solving his murder. In August 1999, a cold case team obtained an exhumation order and finally found the evidence on Justin's body that would nail his killer – a DNA match to Wayne Garrison.

Garrison went on trial for Justin Wiles's murder in November 2001 and, despite his denials, was convicted and sentenced to death.

The conviction was later upheld on appeal although the court decided to vacate the death sentence, citing ineffective assistance from counsel. Then, in October 2006, a district judge overturned the original verdict.

Facing the very real prospect of a three-time child killer back on the streets, prosecutors had to act fast. Garrison was presented with a take-it-or-leave-it offer. Plead guilty, accept life without parole, or go into the new trial with the prospect of the death penalty over your head. He took the deal, although only if he could enter an Alford plea, effectively no contest to the charges. Now serving life with no prospect of parole in an Oklahoma prison, Wayne Garrison continues to insist that he did not murder Justin Wiles.

Shawn Grate

On September 13, 2016, a 911 operator in Ashland, Ohio, received a frantic call. It came from a woman who claimed that she was being held against her will in a vacant house, had been serially raped, and feared that her abductor was planning to kill her. Units were immediately dispatched to the location and found the woman and her kidnapper, a 40-year-old local man named Shawn Grate. He was immediately arrested but appeared unperturbed by the police attention. According to Grate, the woman was his girlfriend and they had plans to marry.

This was clearly not the case, but as the police were about to discover, kidnapping and rape were only a small part of Shawn Grate's criminal repertoire. A search of the house turned up the corpses of two women, both of whom had been strangled. They would soon be identified as Stacey Stanley and Elizabeth Griffith. Stacey had last been seen alive at a Wal-Mart store a month earlier. Elizabeth had disappeared from a BP station in Ashland just the previous week. The Ashland police had just captured a serial killer.

But the addition of two murders to his burgeoning rap sheet did nothing to Shawn Grate's chirpy demeanor. He continued laughing, continued smiling, continued joking with police officers. In fact, he suggested that they might be interested in resolving another unsolved case and, in the days that followed, led them to a burned out house in neighboring Richland County. There, they recovered the corpse of Candice Cunningham, another young woman who had recently disappeared. The discovery left detectives wondering: Just who was Shawn Grate and how many women had he murdered?

Shawn Grate was born on August 8, 1976, in Marion, Ohio. His parents divorced when he was just six years old with his mother getting custody. In his late teens, he was sent to live with his father. By then, he was already a handsome, athletic, and outgoing young man, whose good looks won him many female admirers. He was also showing the traits that would lead him to serial murder.

In November 1994, during his senior year at high school, Grate was arrested for assaulting his girlfriend. This would become a recurring theme throughout his life. In 1996, he choked a 17-year-old until she blacked out. The girl was pregnant with his child at the time. Two months later, he broke into the same young woman's house and threatened her and her sister with a knife. Six months after that, he caused actual harm, inflicting a serious wound on the girl's hand during a struggle. This incident saw him sent him to prison for a second time (he'd previously done time for burglary). It was after his release from this term that Grate's misogynistic violence escalated into murder.

On March 10, 2007, the skeleton of an unidentified young woman was found in Marion County, Ohio. This woman has never been identified, and her fate might have remained a mystery had Grate not admitted to the murder after his arrest. According to him, the victim's name was Dana and she was killed in 2005. This ties in with the date estimated by the medical examiner. It has also been noted that Grate was living in the area at the time.

If Grate is telling the truth, then Dana was his first victim. Nearly ten years would pass before he claimed his second. During that time, Grate married and fathered his second child, although the marriage would last less than two years before his wife divorced him, citing physical abuse. She also had to obtain a restraining order after Grate threatened to kill her and her family.

On January 22, 2015, a young woman named Rebekah Leicy disappeared from Mansfield, Ohio. When her body was found 15 months later, near Mifflin, it was thought that she had died of a drug overdose. That is, until Shawn Grate admitted to her murder. According to Grate, he met Rebecca in a bar and killed her because she stole $4 from him.

Over the next eighteen months, Grate would commit at least two more murders, killing Elizabeth Griffith and Stacey Stanley. The brave young woman who escaped his clutches to call 911 would undoubtedly have become Grate's sixth victim, and there may well be others, still out there. Who knows how many have met their fate at Shawn Grate's strangling hands?

FOOTNOTE: At the time of writing, Shawn Grate is awaiting trial for the Griffin/Stanley murders. The prosecutor has made it clear that he intends seeking the death penalty, but Grate appears unperturbed by the prospect and has continued boasting to the media about his misdeeds.

Thomas Hawkins

When a seasoned County prosecutor labels a killer as "the most calculating, evil criminal that I have encountered in 23 years in law enforcement," you know that you are dealing with a particularly heinous psychopath. And Thomas Hawkins Jr. certainly fits the bill. A man of considerable intelligence, Hawkins is a student of the "art" of murder. When captured, he was found to be in possession of piles of true detective magazines in which he had highlighted passages dealing with killing techniques and ways of avoiding detection. He is also the killer of at least three young women. Given his warped psychology and the period for which he was at large, it is probable that there are other victims besides those three.

Hawkins began his murderous career early, committing his first murder when he was just 16 years old. That was in 1980, when he broke into the girls' dormitory at an exclusive private school in Douglass Township, Pennsylvania, and attacked 15-year-old Karen Stubbs. The teenager was subjected to a vicious rape, then strangled to death and stabbed in the neck with a paint scraper. Arrested soon after, Hawkins was allowed to plead to third-degree murder and sentenced to a 15-year prison term. He served just five years before being paroled in 1986. Three years later, he would kill again.

The victim this time was Andrea Thomas, Hawkins's 14-year-old niece. Andrea's brutalized body was found at the home of Hawkins's parents in West Pottsgrove, Pennsylvania, on June 4, 1989. She had been raped, then strangled with a cord and stabbed in the neck and back with a fork. As a convicted sex offender living in the residence at the time, Thomas Hawkins Jr. was an obvious suspect. However, he'd gone to great lengths to conceal his involvement, ransacking the house to make it look like it had been burgled and building an elaborate alibi for himself. Perhaps too elaborate. Once it was found to be a lie, Hawkins was arrested and charged.

Convicted of first-degree murder at his August 1990 trial, Thomas Hawkins Jr. was sentenced to death. That conviction would later be overturned on a technicality. However, the jury at the 1994 re-trial reached the same conclusion, and Hawkins saw himself returned to death row. By then, he had been connected to a third murder.

Dawn Mozino was 23 years old when she disappeared from a bus stop near the Bryn Mawr Hospital in western Philadelphia on May 22, 1989. Dawn was learning disabled but loved working in the nutrition department of the hospital and also competing in Special Olympics. She'd recently won a medal at the 1989 Lake Tahoe games and was justifiably proud of her achievement. Standing just 4-foot-10 and weighing in at 100 pounds, Dawn looked more like a teenager than a grown woman. She was also known to be an outgoing and happy person, although somewhat naïve due to her disability. That, unfortunately, made her the ideal prey for a predator.

So what connected Hawkins to Dawn's disappearance and probable murder? Firstly, he knew Dawn. They had once been co-workers at Paoli Hospital, and he had recently asked for her help in getting him a job at Bryn Mawr. Second, he was picked out of a photo array by a hospital employee as the man seen talking to Dawn at the bus stop shortly before she went missing. Third, fibers that matched Dawn's hospital uniform were found in his car. This led investigators to surmise that he might have lured her by offering her a ride to the YMCA in Paoli, where she was due to attend athletics practice. Three decades later, Dawn Mozino has still not been found.

And yet, despite now occupying a cell on death row at Graterford Prison, Hawkins has steadfastly refused to admit to Dawn's murder or to tell investigators where he hid her body. This behavior is typical of serial killers. They love to exert control by offering or withholding information. As one investigator wryly commented: "A young woman disappears shortly after being seen in the company of a two-time killer of young women. It doesn't take a genius to connect the dots."

Ivan Hill

Over a ten-week period, between November 1993 and February 1994, the bodies of African-American women began showing up along a 30-mile stretch of State Route 60, between the cities of Ontario and Industry, California. All of the victims were prostitutes and all had been strangled, their bodies discarded in parks, in parking lots, or simply left by the roadside. Given the consistency of the M.O., there were strong suggestions that a serial killer was responsible, although the police initially denied this. Then came a call on December 30, 1993, directing officers to the body of a third victim, Cheryl Sayers. "Y'all better catch me before I kill again," the killer boasted. Shortly after, the press started calling him the "60 Freeway Slayer."

At least five more victims would fall prey to this unnamed fiend over the next six weeks. Yet, despite the brazen nature of the murders, the police could not snare their man. Then the murders suddenly stopped and the case went cold, leaving investigators to conclude that the killer had either left the area, had died, or was in prison on another charge. Serial killers hardly ever stop killing of their own volition.

Fast forward to 2003 and cold case investigators were looking into the case when they got a DNA hit on a man named Ivan Hill. Hill was a career criminal who had previously done time for murder, after he gunned down a liquor store clerk during a holdup. At the time of the freeway killings, he'd been working a number of low-paying jobs in the area of Pomona, California. That put him right at the epicenter of the murders.

Hill wasn't hard to find. He was serving a jail term for yet another armed robbery. Confronted with DNA evidence linking him to six of the murders, Hill did not deny his involvement. In fact, he seemed almost keen to describe how he'd cruised the regular pick-up spots around Mission and Holt Avenues in Pomona; how he'd picked up women for sex; how he'd driven them to isolated spots and then strangled them to death, sometimes with a ligature, sometimes with his bare hands. Betty Sue Harris, Roxanne Bates, Helen Hill, Donna Goldsmith, Cheryl Sayers, Debra Brown and two other unnamed victims had all met a horrible death in this way. Some had been found with duct tape over their mouths, others with their ankles or wrists bound. At least six of the murdered women could be definitely linked to Hill by DNA evidence.

But while Hill was willing to admit to the murders, his defense team argued that there was sufficient mitigation to spare him from the death penalty. The second oldest of five children, Hill had endured terrible abuse at the hands of his father, William. It began when he was just a few weeks old and his father placed a pillow over his face to stop him crying. He might well have been asphyxiated had his mother not intervened.

As Ivan grew, he was subjected to ever more vicious beatings, often delivered with a belt or tree branch and usually for minor infractions. Matters eventually came to a head on Christmas night 1968, when Ivan was 7 years old. That was when his mother, Bessie, tried to intervene on his behalf. In response, William Hill fetched his .22-caliber rifle and shot her in the face. That incident landed William in jail and Bessie in the hospital, fighting for her life. She would eventually recover but, even then, she refused to press charges against her husband. And so William came back home and the abuse continued.

This story was retold at trial by Bessie Hill as she pleaded with the jury to spare her son's life. She also told another macabre tale. In order to give Ivan a break from the regular beatings, she'd sometimes sent him to live with his grandparents. But Ivan's grandmother had one peculiar quirk. She liked to visit the local funeral home to look at dead bodies, and usually she'd take Ivan with her. "Perhaps that was where he developed this obsession with death," Bessie suggested.

It was a heartfelt plea but one that was never likely to work given the crimes that Ivan Hill stood accused of. He was sentenced to death on March 22, 2007, and currently awaits execution.

Robert Hohenberger

Morgan City is a picturesque little burg that sits on the banks of the Atchafalaya River in St. Mary Parish, Louisiana. With a population of just over 12,000, it is a peaceful enclave, low in crime, generally a good place to raise a family. But for three terrifying months in 1978, the city lived under a state of virtual siege. A serial killer was stalking its streets, snatching young girls in broad daylight. By the time he was done, five would be dead, raped and strangled, their bodies disposed of in the most disrespectful way.

No one knows for sure what turned Robert Carl Hohenberger from a California police officer to a heartless killer. But Hohenberger had always played fast and loose with his authority, using his badge to ends that were not entirely legal. Eventually, he started employing it as a tool to lure young women, raping at least four of them before he was arrested and charged. Then, while awaiting trial in California, he staged a daring escape and fled east, ending up in Morgan City. Soon he was staking out the city's shopping malls and public schools, trawling for victims.

The first Morgan City teenager to fall victim to Robert Hohenberger was 16-year-old Mary Leah Rodermund, who disappeared on her way to a drug store in March of 1978. Shortly after, Leah's parents received a call from her abductor, demanding a ransom for her safe return. He even put Leah on the phone to talk to them. Leah's distraught parents never heard from her abductor again.

Over the next two months, two more young girls were snatched, both of them taken from busy public places during daylight hours. In these cases, there were no ransom calls. The girls' bodies would later be found, weighed down and callously discarded in a septic tank. Autopsies on the victims suggested that they had been raped and tortured before being strangled to death.

By now, the city was on high alert, with parents ferrying their children to and from school and extra-curricular activities, and many young women going around armed. Consensus among the locals was that the killer must be an outsider, and local counselors agreed. They quickly passed an ordinance requiring all transients to report to the police for registration and fingerprinting.

Under these conditions, it seemed impossible that the killer could strike again, but he did, abducting 15-year old Judy Adams and 14-year-old Bertha Gould from a high school fair on May 11. This time, however, he'd slipped up. A group of boys had seen him talking to his two victims and thought that they'd seen him flash a police badge at the girls. That explained to investigators how he had so easily gained control over his victims. Even more importantly, the boys were able to provide a description of the man they'd seen. That description would lead to the identification of Robert Hohenberger as the suspect they were seeking.

Unfortunately, Hohenberger had already skipped town. By the time the Morgan City police started their search for him, he was on the other side of the country in Tacoma, Washington. And he would undoubtedly have continued his killing spree, had the Washington State Police not received a tip-off that he was in the area.

Hohenberger was placed under surveillance before police moved in to arrest him on July 15, 1978. However, he was not about to surrender without a fight, and a scuffle ensued. During that altercation, a gun went off, killing Hohenberger on the spot. Some reports suggest that he deliberately shot himself. Whatever the case, he took his deadly secrets with him to the grave. Of the five teenaged girls Hohenberger is known to have killed, Leah Rodermund and Bertha Gould have never been found.

William Howell

On July 31, 2003, a woman walked into a police station in New Britain, Connecticut, and reported that her sister, Nilsa Arizmendi, was missing. On hearing the missing woman's name, the police had a ready suspect. Arizmendi was a prostitute and heroin user, and her boyfriend was a known drug dealer with a violent streak. He had beaten her in the past. Brought in for questioning, however, the boyfriend denied involvement. He offered an alternate suspect, a man named William Devin Howell. According to him, he and Nilsa had allowed Howell to stay in their motel room on July 25. He'd left Nilsa and Howell alone in the room at around 2:30 a.m. that morning. That was the last time he'd seen her alive.

To the police, this sounded like a clear case of shifting the blame. But the boyfriend volunteered for a polygraph...and passed. He was then allowed to go. Investigators now focused their attention on William Howell. After tracking him to his home in Windsor, they executed a search warrant on his van and soon found dried blood under the carpet. Subjected to DNA analysis, it returned a match to two people. Nilsa Arizmendi was one of them.

Howell, however, had an explanation for the presence of the missing woman's blood. He said that Nilsa's boyfriend had slapped her during an argument in the van. The police didn't believe his story. With Nilsa's body still unaccounted for, they decided to charge Howell with manslaughter.

Initially, Howell was adamant that he was innocent and stated his intention to fight the charge. However, as his court date approached, he had a change of heart. In January 2007, he copped an Alford plea, pleading no contest and accepting a 15-year term. He'd later claim that he had only entered the plea under pressure from his public defender.

Just weeks into his jail term, however, William Howell's denials would be exposed as a lie and his monstrous persona would be laid bare for all to see. That was when a hunter was scouting some land behind the West Falls shopping mall in New Britain and came across the decomposed remains of three women – Diane Cusack, Joyvaline Martinez, and Mary Jane Menard. All three were local women who had disappeared four years earlier in mid-2003, and at least one of them had been seen getting into William Howell's blue van.

Confronted by the discovery, Howell continued to plead his innocence, at least to the police. The story he told his cellmate was somewhat different. He described himself as a "sick ripper" with a monster living inside of him. He also said that there were more victims than the three that had been found thus far. And he shared details about the killings, including one particularly macabre tale about how he'd kept a woman's corpse in his van for two weeks because the ground was too frozen for him to bury her. During that time, he'd cuddled up to the corpse at night and called her his "baby."

The police weren't sure what to make of Howell's jailhouse confession. They'd gone over the land behind the mall, an area that Howell called his "garden," and found nothing. Then again, it was difficult terrain, densely wooded, marshy and inaccessible by vehicle. Perhaps there were bodies out there, and perhaps they would eventually turn up.

In fact, it would be eight years before investigators were finally able to verify Howell's jailhouse boasts. That was when they found a cluster of four more corpses – Melanie Ruth Camilini, Marilyn Gonzalez, Janice Roberts, and the victim that had landed Howell in trouble in the first place, Nilsa Arizmendi. Three of the women were prostitutes or had substance abuse problems. One, Janice Roberts, was transgender and also went by the name Danny Lee Whistnant. Howell had told his cellmate that he'd tried to have sex with Roberts but had killed her when he'd found out she was really a man.

William Howell would ultimately plead guilty to six counts of murder and receive six consecutive life sentences. At trial, he made a tearful apology to his victims' families and said that he deserved the death penalty. Unfortunately, the state of Connecticut had repealed that sanction in 2012, after putting to death serial killer Michael Ross. Ross killed six women in Connecticut during the early 80s. Howell exceeded his total by one and is the state's most prolific serial killer.

Bennett Clark Hyde

Born in Cowper, Missouri, in 1872, Bennett Clark Hyde was the son of a Baptist minister. He grew to be an intelligent boy, eventually attending medical school and graduating from a Kansas City college in the mid-1890s. Thereafter, he decided to open a practice in that city, launching a career that was dogged by controversy from the very start. There were allegations of sexual abuse by female patients and an arrest for complicity in a grave-robbing scheme. But those charges were eventually dropped, and Hyde went on to become Kansas City's police surgeon. He was fired from that job in 1907 over accusations of patient abuse. Shortly after, the womanizing doctor announced his betrothal to a young debutant named Frances Swope.

Frances was most definitely not Dr. Hyde's type. In truth, she was rather homely, hardly a match for the dashing doctor. But she was a member of the city's richest and most powerful dynasty, and therein lay the attraction. Her family, of course, was against the union. Not a single member of the Swope clan was in attendance when Bennett and Frances wed in 1907.

But Dr. Hyde's new in-laws were forced to reassess their opinion of him over the years that followed. Quite clearly, he was devoted to his young bride; quite clearly, she was besotted with him. Little by little, he won them over. By 1909, he'd been accepted into the fold. He even became the de facto family physician.

In September of 1909, Dr. Hyde was summoned to the bedside of James Hunton, first cousin to the family patriarch, Colonel Thomas Swope. Hunton had a minor stomach complaint for which Hyde prescribed a couple of pills. A short while after taking them, the patient complained of numbness in his extremities. He then started to suffer convulsions. Within twenty minutes, he had died in agony. Dr. Hyde recorded the cause of death as apoplexy.

A few days later, Hyde was called to attend to Colonel Swope himself. Swope had suffered a minor injury in a fall but had developed gastric problems while bedridden. Hyde provided a couple of "digestion pills" that turned out to be fatal. Colonel Swope died of symptoms that were remarkably similar to those suffered by his cousin. Cause of death was again listed as apoplexy.

Now a curse seemed to descend on the Swope clan. Several developed gastric problems, and eight family members, all named as beneficiaries in Colonel Swope's will, were struck down by typhoid. One of them, Chrisman Swope, died of the disease on December 6. That prompted Hyde's mother-in-law to contact the police and voice her suspicions. She believed that Dr. Hyde was systematically killing off members of her family in order to lay claim to the substantial fortune left behind by Colonel Swope.

This was a serious allegation with not much evidence to back it up. Nonetheless, the authorities decided to exhume Colonel Swope and his nephew, Chrisman, for autopsy. The results were inconclusive. Small traces of strychnine were found but not in concentrations significant enough to cause death. Dr. Hyde was off the hook.

His reprieve, however, would be short-lived. A few days later, one of Hyde's colleagues came forward to inform the police that Hyde had removed a test tube containing typhoid cultures from their shared laboratory. Since eight members of the Swope family had contracted typhoid just days later, and one had died, this was interesting information. In late December 1909, Hyde was arrested and charged with murder.

The trial, beginning on April 11, 1910, once again pitted Frances Swope against her family. While Frances stood by her husband, several members of the Swope clan testified that they'd become ill after taking capsules given to them by Hyde. One witness even contended that Hyde had jabbed her with a needle while she slept. The defense responded by asserting that the family had become ill after drinking contaminated water. That, however, did not account for the deaths of Colonel Swope and James Hunton. Found guilty of three counts of murder, Bennett Clark Hyde was sentenced to life in prison.

The sentence, of course, went on appeal, with Frances Hyde fighting her husband's corner over three more trials, eventually securing his acquittal in 1917. Her devotion would go unrewarded. Just three years after that court victory, she filed for divorce, citing "repeated and constant acts of cruelty and violence." Perhaps her family had been right all along.

Bennett Clark Hyde lived out the rest of his life in relative anonymity in the small town of Lexington, Missouri. He died suddenly on August 8, 1934. Ironically, his cause of death was listed as "apoplexy," the diagnosis he'd so often applied to his patients.

Wilbur Jennings

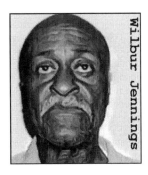

Between August 1993 and December 1994, police in Fresno, California were hunting a particularly vicious serial killer. The killer had a clearly defined M.O. He mainly targeted black prostitutes, luring them to one of the many canals in the county, raping them, beating them, and then throwing them into the water. Some died from the savage blows he delivered. Others survived the beating but were too weak to swim to safety and thus drowned.

The first woman to fall prey to this predator was 21-year-old Karen Robinson, whose body was discovered in an irrigation pond near Easton on August 23, 1983. Eleven months later, 21-year-old Jacqueline Frazier was found in a canal in Caruthers, and just three weeks after that, Linda Johnson, 28, was pulled from the water in San Joaquin. Unlike the other victims, Johnson was not a prostitute. She had apparently been snatched from a Fresno street. And neither was she the last of the so-called Ditch Bank Killer's victims. On December 18, he struck again, drowning 23-year-old Olga Cannon in an irrigation ditch near Easton.

Four women were dead, brutally slain within the space of just 17 months. But at least there was a solid suspect by now, a local laborer named Wilbur Jennings. It was Jennings's unusual behavior that first brought him to the attention of the police. Standing 6-foot-two and weighing in at 220 pounds, Jennings regularly picked up prostitutes on G Street in Fresno. Often, he didn't want to have sex with them. He just wanted the woman to hold him in her arms and tell him that she loved him. When she did, he'd usually start crying, but if she refused, he'd often become violent.

Jennings was eventually brought in for questioning, and although he denied involvement in the killings, he soon incriminated himself. He was later put on trial, convicted of four murders, and sentenced to death. At the time, investigators stated their belief that he might be responsible for as many as nine homicides.

Fast forward to 2005 and cold case detectives in Fresno County were looking into two very different murders. One involved a 76-year-old widow named Clarice Reinke, the other a teenager named Debra Chandler. What made these cases suitable for re-examination was that semen had been retrieved from the victims and could be sent for DNA analysis. No one had any inkling that the murders might be connected.

Debra Chandler had been killed in Sacramento County on July 4, 1981. On that day, she'd left her family home, saying that she was going to visit a friend. The following morning, a motorist spotted her body lying beside a water-filled roadside ditch, about 15 miles from where she lived. An autopsy would show that she'd been raped and beaten to death.

Clarice Reinke's murder was totally different, and not just because of the 60-year age gap between her and Debra Chandler. The 76-year-old had been found inside her Fresno home, raped, sodomized, and strangled to death. Semen was recovered from the corpse, but at that time, DNA "fingerprinting" was not yet available as an investigative tool. Now it was, although investigators had a two-month wait before they would have the results back. When those results eventually arrived, they were astounding.

First, there were two separate profiles. Second, those profiles were found on both Clarice Reinke and Debra Chandler, thus linking the murders to a common perpetrator. Third, one of the profiles belonged to Wilbur Jennings. That was unusual because these latest victims were far removed from Jennings's preferred targets. They were not prostitutes and, unlike his other victims, they were white.

As for the second DNA profile, it belonged to a man named Alvin Johnson who was serving a prison term in Utah for rape and murder. At the time of the murders, though, Johnson had been living at the Fresno Rescue Mission. The shelter is on G Street, on the same block where Jennings liked to trawl for prostitutes. That is likely where the two men met.

Jennings, however, denied that he knew Johnson. He also denied killing the two women. In fact, while he was at it, he denied the four murders that had sent him to death row in the first place. According to him, he'd been set up. Asked how his DNA might have ended up on the victims, Jennings was in a typically belligerent mood. He described the technology as "a bunch of crap."

Despite his denials, Jennings was eventually arraigned for the Chandler and Reinke murders. But he would never stand trial. He died of prostate cancer in 2014. It remains to be seen whether Alvin Johnson will ever be charged.

Bryan Jones

Between the years 1985 and 1989, San Diego, California experienced a sudden surge in violent crime. Prostitutes and homeless women appeared to be particularly at risk, with at least 45 of these vulnerable individuals killed during this period. In response, city and county officials put together a dedicated investigative team. Called, rather unimaginatively, the San Diego Metropolitan Homicide Task Force, it included officers from San Diego PD, detectives from the sheriff's department, and prosecutors provided by the county. This team would remain in place for four years and would achieve considerable success, bringing any number of miscreants to justice and closing an impressive percentage of the cases assigned to them. By 1989, with the team about to be disbanded, they were justifiably proud of what they'd accomplished.

And yet, one particular set of murders still rankled with investigators. On August 29, 1985, police and firefighters had responded to a report of a fire in an alley off 51st Street. They arrived to find a blazing dumpster, from which they later retrieved the body of 18-year-old prostitute, Tara Simpson. An autopsy would reveal that she'd been raped, sodomized, stabbed in the stomach, and strangled. If there was one small mercy, it was that she'd been dead by the time her killer doused her with lighter fluid and set her alight.

Five months later, on February 11, 1986, firefighters responded to another funeral pyre in the same alley. The victim was another prostitute, 22-year-old Trina Carpenter. She'd been strangled to death. This time at least, someone had seen something. An eyewitness reported spotting a light blue vehicle parked in the alley shortly before the fire started. He said that it was "sporty-looking" and "possibly foreign," although he couldn't be certain.

On May 9, 1986, two months after the murder of Trina Carpenter, police officers were called to the scene of yet another murder in the 51st Street alley. Unlike the previous two victims, JoAnn Sweets had not been set alight. She had, however, been sodomized and strangled to death, and the proximity of the body to the other two victims suggested that the same killer was responsible.

And the same man would commit a fourth murder, just three months later, although in this case, the connection was not immediately obvious. The victim was a 37-year-old homeless woman and occasional prostitute named Sophia Glover. She was found wrapped in a blanket and left on a grassy sidewalk on Madison Avenue in the Normal Heights area of the city. Cause of death, however, was the same. She'd died from manual strangulation. She'd also been raped and sodomized.

For the members of the task force, this was the killer that had eluded them, the one that got away. They were certain that a single perpetrator was responsible for all four murders and had worked the case hard. Yet for all their efforts, they'd come up empty. A serial killer had slipped through their grasp. It was very frustrating.

Unbeknownst to the investigators, they already had their suspect in custody. His name was Bryan Maurice Jones and he was serving a 22-year prison term for sexual assault. He was also due in court on two additional rapes charges investigated by the task force. It was only when prosecutors began preparing for trial that the pieces started falling into place. Jones lived just a stone's throw from the first three murder scenes; he often stayed with a relative close to the fourth murder scene. He also had access to a vehicle that matched the one seen in the alleyway. It was a light blue Datsun 280-Z and it belonged to his sister. Jones, however, often borrowed the car.

With a suspect now in their sights, the task team turned to forensics to build their case. It wasn't that difficult. Fibers from Jones's mattress and bedding were found on the victims; fibers from their clothes were found in his car; his fingerprints were found on a plastic bag used to conceal JoAnn Sweets's body; the blanket wrapped around Sophia Glover turned out to belong to Jones's mother. And that was even before the sperm lifted from the victims was matched to their killer.

It all added up to a case that Bryan Jones had no chance of beating. Found guilty at trial, he was sentenced to death. The San Diego

Metropolitan Homicide Task Force had saved its biggest win for last.

Jeffrey Jones

Born in Sacramento, California, in 1960, Jeffrey Jones had an apparently happy childhood and did well at school. It was only while attending college in Arizona that evidence of his bizarre persona began to emerge. Eventually, his behavioral problems became so extreme he was ejected from the university. Thereafter, the now 22-year-old Jones returned home, where his concerned parents sent him to see a psychiatrist. As a result of those sessions, he was diagnosed with chronic paranoid schizophrenia and placed on anti-psychotic medication.

And for a while, that seemed to work. But then, one night in early 1984, John Jones awoke to find his son standing beside his bed, holding a large kitchen knife. It was a sign of things to come. By May of that year, Jeffrey had been arrested for the knifepoint robbery of a disabled man. He pled not guilty by reason of insanity and, regrettably, the Yolo County court system decided to go easy on him. He was given probation and ordered to stay on his medication. That leniency would turn out to be a tragic mistake.

Shortly after noon on January 18, 1985, a university professor named James McClain entered a restroom on the campus of the University of California in Davis and found his colleague, Professor Fred Morris, lying on the floor near the urinals in a pool of blood. McClain immediately summoned help, but by the time it arrived, Morris was already dead, having suffered multiple blunt force trauma injuries to his head. These were circular and about an inch in diameter, suggesting that they had been inflicted by a hammer.

The dust had not yet settled on the campus murder when there was another, this time at Sutter's Fort, near Sacramento. At around midday on January 21, a man entered a restroom at the location. He was carrying a claw hammer and intent on doing harm to anyone he encountered. That unfortunate individual turned out to be Henry Dong, who was brutally attacked, his head pulverized in a frenzied onslaught. Dong was discovered soon after and was rushed to hospital. But there was very little that could be done for him. In the words of one first responder, his head and face were "pretty much destroyed."

And the killer was not done yet. At around 5:00 p.m. that same afternoon, he was back on the UC campus. There, he cornered medical student John Rowland in a restroom and attacked, battering the young man to a pulp. Rowland was left for dead but somehow managed to pull himself into the corridor to summon help. That act of superhuman determination undoubtedly saved Rowland's life although he would have to undergo a series of operations to repair fractures that ran from the back of his head to his right jaw. Even then, he was left with balance and hearing problems and paralysis to one side of his face. The next victim would not be so lucky.

On the late afternoon of January 22, just a day after the double hammer attack, an intern was passing a restroom at the Sacramento Medical Center when he heard a scream. As Ron English approached the door, an African-American man emerged. English asked whether he was okay. The man replied that he was but that someone inside was injured. He then brushed past English and pushed his way through the crowd that had started to form in the corridor. When he took off running, English bravely gave chase, eventually tackling him to the ground and holding him until the campus police arrived. The man was then cuffed and taken into custody. A bloody claw hammer was found in one of his pockets. While all of this was going on, another student had entered the restroom and found Dr. Michael Corbett lying gravely injured on the floor. Despite desperate efforts to save him, Corbett died later that night.

By now, the suspect had been identified as Jeffrey Jones and the evidence had already started stacking up against him. The hammer he was carrying corresponded to the injuries inflicted on all four victims. Meanwhile, blood found on his clothing was matched to Corbett, Rowland, and Dong. Despite this, Jones initially insisted that he had been framed. He later changed his tune and entered a plea of "not guilty by reason of insanity." It didn't work. Found guilty on two counts of first-degree murder and one count of attempted murder, he was sentenced to death.

Todd Kohlhepp

Like most serial killers, Todd Kohlhepp showed signs of his warped personality at an early age. Even at nursery school, he proved impossible to control, constantly bullying the other children and stealing or destroying their property. And those problems would only increase as he grew older. He quickly developed a temper and a precocious interest in sex. He also started showing a trait common to psychopaths – cruelty to animals. He enjoyed taking potshots at the family dog with a BB gun and once poisoned a bowl of goldfish by pouring Clorox into their water. That incident saw him sent for psychological evaluation, and he ended up spending three months in a Georgia mental hospital. On his release, his mother packed him off to live with his biological father in Arizona.

But Kohlhepp Sr. was hardly the best role model. He was obsessed with guns and taught his son how to shoot and how to "make bombs and blow up things." He also left Todd to his own devices for long periods of time while he took off with various girlfriends. Perhaps unsurprisingly, the boy (who had a high average IQ of 118) dropped out of school and started working a series of menial jobs. It was around this time that he committed his first serious offense.

On November 25, 1986, 15-year-old Todd Kohlhepp kidnapped a 14-year-old girl at gunpoint, brought her back to his father's house and raped her. He then released his victim, warning her that he'd kill her younger siblings if she said anything to the police. Despite this threat, the girl did report the rape and Kohlhepp was arrested and charged with kidnapping and sexual assault. He later struck a deal, pleading guilty to kidnapping in exchange for the rape charge being dropped. The kidnapping conviction was enough to earn him a 15-year term.

Kohlhepp would serve all but one year of his sentence. Paroled in August 2001, he moved back to South Carolina to be near his mother. While in prison, he had obtained a bachelor's degree in computer science, and he now supplemented it with a business administration degree from the University of South Carolina Upstate. In 2006, he obtained a real estate license and started a company that would eventually employ a dozen agents. He also got a private pilot's license and bought several parcels of land, including nearly 100 acres near Moore, South Carolina. On the surface, it appeared that Todd Kohlhepp had turned his life around.

What was going on below the surface, though, was quite different. Kohlhepp was still a conflicted man. He could be charming when he wanted to be, but he still had that explosive temper and that underlying narcissism. He also maintained his obsession with sex... and with firearms.

On August 31, 2016, 30-year-old Kala Brown and her boyfriend, Charles David Carver, 32, went missing. Since the couple had occasionally worked for Kohlhepp, he was questioned regarding their whereabouts and denied knowing anything. Detectives weren't sure that they believed him, but they couldn't prove otherwise. That is, until November 3, when officers acted on a tip-off and found Kala Brown chained up in a metal container on Kohlhepp's property. The unfortunate woman had been held as a prisoner for over two months. She was able to describe to detectives how Kohlhepp had gunned down her boyfriend. She also led officers to a gravesite that Kohlhepp had shown her. There, they uncovered the bodies of Johnny Joe Coxie, 29, and his wife Meagan, 26, former employees of Kohlhepp, who had been reported missing on December 22, 2015.

And even that wasn't the full extent of Todd Kohlhepp's murderous activities. Investigators also linked him to a quadruple shooting at a motorcycle workshop in 2003. Kohlhepp had apparently enquired about buying a Harley but his inability to maintain his balance on the machine had brought laughter from the employees. Their hilarity would end up costing their lives. Humiliated, Kohlhepp drew a pistol and gunned down all four of them.

Questioned by detectives, Todd Kohlhepp made no attempt to deny the charges against him. Indeed, he seemed more than willing to talk about the murders, even hinting that there are others, yet to be discovered. He remains the prime suspect in a shooting in Tempe, Arizona, and in a triple homicide in Greer,

South Carolina. For now, he has copped a plea to seven counts of murder and accepted seven consecutive life sentences without the possibility of parole. This story, most likely, has not run its course.

David Lucas

Prosecutor Daniel Williams called them "the most vicious and cold-blooded murders San Diego has ever had to suffer." And he may well be right. How else would you categorize a double homicide in which a young mother and her three-year-old toddler had their throats savagely cut? Suzanne Jacobs and her son, Colin, had been slaughtered in their Normal Heights home on May 4, 1979, the cuts so deep that they had almost been decapitated. It had taken the authorities ten years to finally put their alleged killer, David Lucas, in front of a jury. And Lucas had not been idle during the intervening years.

Like many serial killers, David Allen Lucas had endured a difficult path through life. An asthma sufferer as a child, he'd also have to endure the attentions of a demanding, workaholic father who beat him frequently. This treatment caused Lucas to be both a bed-wetter and a thumb-sucker, habits which continued well into his teens and earned him repeated physical and verbal abuse. Still, there were some positive aspects to the boy's life. He was a regular churchgoer and was proud to be an altar boy. And unlike most fledgling serial killers, he apparently loved animals.

Then, in 1970, came the incident that would turn David Lucas's life on its head. A girl he'd been dating announced that she was pregnant, and even as an unwed 16-year-old, Lucas was thrilled at the prospect of becoming a father. He was devastated when his girlfriend had an abortion without telling him. From then on, Lucas developed a love/hate relationship with women, a warped worldview that regarded females as both nurturing and treacherous. When he eventually married and fathered a child, he would frequently accuse his wife of abusing their baby, even though this was clearly not the case.

How this protective attitude toward children tallies with slashing a three-year-old's throat is difficult to fathom. It is also difficult to understand why Lucas apparently went into a four-and-a-half-year hiatus after the frenzied double murder of Suzanne and Colin Jacobs. Perhaps he felt remorse over the murder of the child. Whatever the case, by 1984, the killer inside David Lucas was back in control. This time, he'd unleash an unprecedented orgy of violence.

In June of that year, 34-year-old Jodie Santiago Robertson was walking home from a nightclub in La Mesa, California, when she was snatched from the street and forced into a car. Her abductor then drove to an isolated area where he dragged Jodie from the vehicle and slashed her across the throat before driving off. He probably thought that his victim would bleed to death. Miraculously, no vital blood vessels had been severed and Jodie Robertson survived.

Rhonda Strang and Amber Fisher were not so lucky. On October 23, 1984, Rhonda was babysitting 3-year-old Amber at her home in Lakeside, a suburb of San Diego. Sometime during the evening, an intruder entered the home and cut the throats of both victims, leaving them to bleed to death at the scene.

And then came the murder that would lead to David Lucas's downfall. On the afternoon of November 20, 1984, University of San Diego honor student, Anne Swanke, was driving along the I-8 near La Mesa, California, when she ran out of gas. Anne then walked to the Grossmont Center Shell station and filled a canister before starting the walk back to her car. She never made it. Her 1974 Dodge Colt was later found abandoned on the freeway. Her body, throat slashed, was discovered four days later in a remote area of Spring Valley.

The murder of Anne Swanke would lead investigators eventually to the door of David Lucas. Then, the forensic pieces started slotting together, linking Lucas to the attempted murder of Jodie Robertson and to the murders of Suzanne and Colin Jacobs, Rhonda Strang and Amber Fisher. There was also another charge, for the December 1981 killing of 29-year-old real estate agent Gayle Garcia. Gayle's body was found in a Spring Valley home that she had been showing to prospective buyers. Her throat had been cut from ear to ear.

In the end, Lucas's various trials delivered the full spectrum of possible results. He was acquitted of the Garcia murder, while the Strang and Fisher trial ended in a hung jury and the Swanke and Jacobs trials in convictions. That was enough to earn Lucas the death penalty. He currently awaits his fate on California's death row at San Quentin.

Victor Malone

To the denizens of Detroit's seedier strip clubs, Victor Malone was a high-roller, a wearer of expensive three-piece suits, a punter who invariably had a fistful of cash and was generous in doling it out. Well-spoken and refined, the college-educated Malone had a master's degree in social science from the University of Michigan. He was, at least to the outside world, a gentleman. Dancers were treated with respect and the management of the clubs he frequented never had a moment's trouble from him. To them, Malone was the perfect customer.

But might there have been a darker side to Victor Malone? A side that he kept hidden from the world? Most of those who knew Malone would have said no. Sure, he did seem to have an abnormally high sex drive, but that was just being a red-blooded male, surely? Since when has possession of an over-developed libido been a crime? When that libido leads to murder, is the answer.

On the evening of July 23, 1984, Victor Malone was working his usual beat, cruising the bars and topless lounges of Detroit's rundown Highland Park neighborhood. This being a Monday, the clubs were less than full, but that did nothing to distract Malone from his revelry. He was in a generous mood, buying drinks and paying two different women to accompany him to private booths for sex. He also got up on stage to engage in a sex act with a dancer.

Yet despite his shenanigans, Malone was left feeling frustrated. This was something he often complained about to staff and other customers. No matter how much debauchery he indulged in, he was always left unfulfilled. On this particular evening, he decided to address the problem by paying dancer and prostitute Anita Willis to accompany him to the nearby Woodward Motel. It was at that same motel that Willis was found the next morning, strangled to death.

Malone, who had rented the motel room in his own name, was questioned, of course. And since there was no point in denying it, he readily admitted paying for the room and being there with the victim. However, he claimed that he'd been unable to perform sexually. He had dropped Willis off at another club, he said, where she was due to meet a client. That was the last time he'd seen her, and she had been very much alive.

The police initially did not believe Malone's story. But once they started questioning staff at the clubs he frequented and started hearing the glowing testimonials about his character, they began to doubt their initial impressions. In any case, they had no physical evidence linking Malone to Anita Willis's death, and so he was allowed to leave.

But then another prostitute connected to Victor Malone turned up strangled to death and thrown into a dumpster. And then there was a third. Leshia Brooks was a dancer at the Fancy Pants Lounge in Highland Park. She was also an occasional prostitute. On the night of December 5, 1984, Brooks finished her stint on stage and got into a conversation with Malone, during which she indicated that she wanted to go to a local dope house to buy some drugs before she was due back on. Malone offered to take her, and the two of them left the club together.

But Brooks never returned. Her nude body was found the next morning, about a block away from the dope house. Malone, who had come back to the club a couple of hours after leaving with Brooks, was an obvious suspect, with investigators noting that he'd recently been interrogated regarding another dead prostitute. Brought in for questioning, Malone offered a similar story to the one he'd told before. He said that he'd dropped Brooks off at the dope house and that she'd been alive and well when he'd left her. This time, however, the police were not prepared to accept his story, and he was arrested and charged with murder. Two additional murder charges would later be added to the rap sheet.

Victor Malone would ultimately be convicted of three counts of second-degree murder and sentenced to 65 to 100 years in prison. He continues to protest his innocence from behind bars, saying that he was convicted because of his lifestyle, rather than evidence of murder. Nonetheless, he has since been linked to ten prostitute murders, committed over a 12-year period. That would make him one of the most prolific killers in Detroit's history.

Chander Matta

On the morning of May 30, 1990, police officers were called to an office complex in west Alexandria where the partially nude body of a young woman had been found. The victim was 16-year-old Jodie Phillips, a novice prostitute who worked the notorious Washington D.C. pick-up area known colloquially as *The Stroll.* But it was the method of murder that most concerned investigators. Jodie Phillips had been asphyxiated by having a plastic shopping bag pulled over her head. She was the third woman to be found in that condition in as many days. It appeared that the capital had a serial killer stalking its streets. One who had already murdered three women.

The other two victims had also been denizens of *The Stroll,* although they'd been on the game longer than Phillips. Twenty-year-old Sandra Rene Johnson had been found suffocated to death in her apartment on May 27; Sherry Larman, 26, had turned up dead a day earlier, her body dumped at a parking garage on the 900 block of South Highland Street in Arlington. Like the other victims, she still had a plastic bag pulled over her head. That pointed to a killer who was both cruel and prolific. According to the medical examiner, the women had all been killed within a 36-hour period over the Memorial Day weekend. Unless he was caught soon, the killer would likely strike again.

But the police were about to receive a massive break in their investigation. Inside the plastic bag that had been used to kill Jodie Phillips, officers found a credit card receipt from an Arlington drugstore. It was for the purchase of garden supplies and had been paid for by a man named Matta. Police were soon able to track the credit card holder to an address in South Arlington, where he shared a neat stone house with his wife and two sons, a teenager and a 22-year-old. They soon learned that Matta was an immigrant from India who was now retired and had no police record whatsoever. Since that made him a very unlikely serial killer, attention fell on his sons, particularly 22-year-old Chander, known to his friends and family as "Bobby."

Bobby Matta was immediately placed under police surveillance. In the meantime, detectives began looking into his background and learned that he was a college dropout currently employed by the Department of Defense as a printer. He also worked a part-time job as a customer service agent for USAir. Detectives learned also that he'd been home alone during the time frame of the murders, since his parents and brother had been out of town. That, at the very least, gave him opportunity. It was therefore decided to bring him in for questioning.

Matta gave very little away during the initial interview, stating quite correctly that anyone could have pulled a plastic bag from his family's trash. Investigators were nonetheless suspicious enough to obtain a search warrant for the Matta residence. The search turned up nothing incriminating. At this stage, it looked like Matta would walk.

But during a second interview, cracks started to show in the young man's demeanor. He was clearly nervous and became increasingly defensive as he was caught in a number of inconsistencies. That gave the interrogators a way in and they did not let it go to waste.

They kept up the pressure. During the third interrogation, Matta eventually broke down and started crying. "I did it," he sobbed pitifully, "I killed them."

According to Matta, the first killing took place on May 26. On that Friday afternoon, he drove to the area of K and 13th streets where he picked up Sherry Larman. The young woman was taken to the Matta residence where she and Matta had sex. Then, as she prepared to leave, he clubbed her from behind and then pulled a bag over her head, holding it in place while she thrashed around in her death throes. "I used a military grip," he proudly told investigators.

But now Matta had a problem, a corpse to dispose of and his shift about to start at USAir. Needing to delay its disposal, he dragged the body down into the basement and then left for work. He'd spend the afternoon cheerfully dispensing advice to customers, while his victim lay dead in his house. Later, after completing his shift, he loaded the corpse into his car and dumped it at an Arlington parking garage, where it would later be found. Just hours later, he was back on *The Stroll*, trawling for his next victim.

That unfortunate woman was teenager Jodie Phillips, who suffered a similar fate to Sherry Larman. This time, Matta subdued his victim by tying her hands behind her back before he snuffed out her life. On his next visit to *The Stroll*, Matta picked up Sandra Johnson, going to her South Arlington apartment rather than bringing her to his home. The outcome was the same, though. Johnson was suffocated and then placed in the bathtub, where she was later found.

Chander Matta did not deny murder at his 1991 trial. His defense attorney did, however, raise an insanity defense, claiming that his client was schizophrenic. The jury rejected that plea and found Matta guilty. He was sentenced to life in prison without parole.

Ynobe Matthews

In the early morning hours of Sunday, May 28, 2000, firefighters in College Station, Texas, responded to a report of a fire at an apartment complex. Arriving on the scene at around 4:50 a.m., the firemen soon tracked the source of the blaze to a particular unit. Smoke was billowing from this apartment through a partially open window. It appeared also that the screen covering of the window had been cut, suggesting a possible break-in. In fact, it was far more serious than that. As firefighters entered the apartment, they found the corpse of a young woman, naked except for a t-shirt and a pair of socks. She was seated on the floor, her back propped up against a bed and her legs spread. A small fire had been started between her legs and had burned her inner thighs and vaginal area, leaving the sickening stench of seared flesh in the air. While one of the firefighters got to work extinguishing the blaze, the other went to call the police.

It did not take long for detectives to establish that this was a rape and murder. The victim, identified as 21-year-old Carolyn Casey, had been strangled, and a ripped pair of panties found nearby suggested a violent sexual assault. It appeared that the killer had then started the fire in order to destroy forensic evidence. The victim's house and car keys were missing but would later be found in a dumpster downstairs.

As detectives began questioning Carolyn Casey's neighbors, they learned that the young woman had attended a party in the building that night. At some point during the evening, she had driven another party-goer to a nearby grocery store to buy more alcohol, but she'd left the festivities soon after returning, saying that she felt unwell. That was at around 1:30 a.m. Shortly thereafter, Carolyn's neighbor had heard a series of loud thumps coming from her apartment, although they'd soon stopped. This was important information, since it pointed to a suspect.

Ynobe Matthews was the man who Carolyn had driven to the grocery store, and other guests recalled that he had been missing from the party at around the time that Carolyn left. Matthews appeared happy to talk to detectives and also to provide samples of his head hair, pubic hair, blood and saliva. He also turned over the clothing that he'd worn to the party, and that was when the investigators' suspicions were really roused. The clothes he'd given them did not match what he was wearing in the surveillance footage from the grocery store.

Confronted with this, Matthews insisted that it was a simple mistake and handed over the correct garments. Those items would return several important clues, including a match to fibers found on Carolyn's skin and under her nails. Matthews's DNA also matched scrapings taken from under Carolyn's fingernails, but

Matthews had a ready explanation for this. He claimed that he and Carolyn had been dating for about a month and that they'd had consensual sex on the night of her death. He'd then left her apartment and gone back to the party.

But the investigators weren't buying that story. They kept pressing until Matthews eventually broke down and confessed. He admitted that he'd choked Carolyn but claimed that it was during an argument over her flirting with other men. He'd then panicked and decided to cover up the crime. First, he slashed the screen to make it look as though someone had broken in. Then he started the fire, hoping to destroy DNA evidence.

This latest story may have been closer to the truth, but it was still a lie. No one in their circle knew of a romantic involvement between Matthews and Carolyn. This was no lovers' tiff gone wrong, this was cold-blooded murder. Matthews had followed Carolyn from the party with the intention of raping her. He'd killed her to cover up the crime. As detectives were soon to discover, she was far from his only victim.

As the matter proceeded towards trial, investigators learned of three brutal rapes committed by Matthews, and two attempted rapes during which he'd punched and choked his victims. A sixth young woman was not so lucky. Twenty-one-year-old Jamie Hart was raped, beaten, and strangled with a ligature before being thrown from a moving vehicle, sustaining road rash injuries and skull fractures that led to her death. Her body was later dumped in a roadside ditch.

DNA would tie Ynobe Matthews to Jamie Hart's murder and also to the deaths of four more women, although he'd never be tried for these crimes. A conviction in the Carolyn Casey homicide was enough to send him to death row. He was put to death by lethal injection on January 6, 2004.

Tom McCormick

Any way you sliced it, Tom McCormick was a successful farmer. McCormick owned one of the largest spreads in Colorado's Kit Carson County, a sprawling 2,900 acres of prime land on which he grew wheat, corn, and soybeans and also raised cattle. But for all his success, McCormick was unpopular with his neighbors. This was hardly surprising when you consider his temperament. He was unfriendly to the point of being anti-social; quarrelsome to the point of being confrontational. Anyone who stepped on his land uninvited was likely to be escorted from the premises at the business end of a shotgun. He also refused to hire locals at harvest time, preferring to drive all the way to Denver to recruit homeless men from a church mission.

These anti-social traits would eventually come back to bite McCormick when financial problems hit in the early eighties. With no support network to turn to, he was forced to sell off large tracts of his land at well under their market value. Driven to the brink of bankruptcy, he cast around for new sources of income and struck on the idea of operating a "chop shop." Soon stolen trucks and cars were rolling onto the McCormick property to be resprayed and to have their serial numbers altered before being sold on. Tom's son Michael was in charge of the operation, and it turned out to be quite a money spinner.

By January 1984, the McCormicks' illicit operation had become big enough to appear on the radar of the state police. However, no action was taken until July of that year when an alert vehicle inspector in Roseburg, Oregon, picked up altered details on a Kenworth tractor-trailer. The new owner swore that he had purchased the vehicle legitimately in Phoenix, Arizona, and that turned out to be true. However, the trail from there got dirty, and it led back to Mike McCormick. Even more interesting was the fact that the registered owner of the vehicle, a 60-year-old trucker named Herbert Donoho, had disappeared from a truck stop in Wheat Ridge, Colorado, back in August 1983. That was when investigators started to suspect that they might have stumbled onto something far more serious than a stolen vehicle.

In June of 1985, various indictments were issued against Mike McCormick, including one for the murder of Herbert Donoho. However, McCormick was one step ahead of the State Police. He fled the jurisdiction before they could take him into custody. He was eventually tracked to Nebraska and arrested in a raid during January 1986. Just weeks later, he struck a deal, offering to unmask a serial killer in exchange for prosecutors not seeking the death penalty against him.

The serial killer that Mike was talking about was his own father, Tom. According to his testimony, it was Tom who had shot

Donoho, killing the trucker in order to steal his rig. However, this wasn't the only murder that Tom McCormick had committed. According to Mike, his father had killed at least seven migrant workers over a period of ten years. The men had been hired to work on the McCormick spread, but Tom had gunned them down rather than pay them. The bodies, according to Mike, were still buried on the property.

On January 30, 1986, Mike McCormick led investigators to a field near Byers, Colorado, where they unearthed the body of Herbert Donoho. Thereafter, Colorado Bureau of Investigation agents descended on the McCormick ranch with heavy earth-moving equipment and started digging. By early February, they had unearthed three skeletons, later identified as Robert Sowarsh, James Sinclair, and James Irvin Plance. Each of the men had been killed by a shotgun blast to the head.

As many as 17 missing men had by now been linked to the McCormick ranch. However, bad weather caused a halt to the evacuations. By the time it cleared, budget constraints and doubts over Mike McCormick's story brought a halt to the evacuations.

Michael McCormick was ultimately convicted of second-degree murder in the Donoho case but was a free man by 2005. In the interim, his father, Tom, had died, breathing his last on November 15, 1997. He was never charged, even though evidence suggests that he might be Colorado's worst ever mass murderer.

Anthony McKnight

On October 5, 1985, 13-year-old Talita Dixon left her home in Oakland, California, and began her short walk to school. Today was a big day for Talita, the first day on which she'd make the walk alone. Previously, her mother had always accompanied her, but she was a teenager now and embarrassed by having a minder. And so today she was flying solo for the first time... and also the last. Three days later, on October 8, a jogger found Talita's body near a foot path in the Oakland Hills. She'd been raped, beaten and stabbed repeatedly. Her neck was broken and an arm had been ripped from her body. It was almost as though she'd been killed by a wild beast rather than a man.

But, as savage as Talita's murder was, it was not the first that Oakland PD had to deal with that year. Neither would it be the last. Between September and December, four more victims would turn up dead, all of them young women. Seventeen-year-old Diane Stone was killed before Talita Dixon, while the deaths of Monique Davis, 18, Beverly Ann Bryant, 24, and Betty Lynn Stuart, 22, would follow. Given the violence perpetrated on the bodies, the police were in no doubt that the same man was responsible.

And yet, for all the man hours expended on the case, the police were coming up empty in their search for the killer. They had physical evidence in the form of semen lifted from the victims, but in those pre-DNA days, that was of little use in identifying a suspect. All they could do was to work the angles and hope that something broke for them before he killed again. And he would kill again. Of that, they were certain.

At the same time, the Oakland police were investigating another high profile case, this one involving a serial rapist. This suspect appeared to be a particularly cruel individual who enjoyed playing a "cat and mouse game" with his victims. Sometimes he'd allow them to escape, only to hunt them down again and subject them to more torment. Victims were raped, sodomized, forced to perform oral sex. Some were even stabbed.

But at least they were alive and able to provide a description of their attacker. Those descriptions led police eventually to 32-year-old Anthony McKnight, an enlisted man based at the Alameda Naval Air Station. McKnight was brought in for questioning but appeared, at first, to be an unlikely rapist. He was a married man with a baby daughter; neighbors in his building called him friendly, helpful, and outgoing; his supervisors said that he was reliable and trustworthy.

These glowing character references, though, did not tell the full story. Anthony McKnight had been living a double life and evidence of his crimes quickly began stacking up against him. Once his victims picked him out of a police lineup, McKnight was charged with rape, sodomy, and attempted murder. He'd eventually be convicted and sentenced to 23 years in prison.

But were these the only crimes that Anthony McKnight was guilty of? The law officers who had interviewed him thought not. They believed that he was the man responsible for the five unsolved murders, and that belief was given credence when the killings stopped right after his arrest. The problem was that McKnight denied murder, and there was no solid evidence linking him to the crimes.

Fast forward just a short time to 1999, and by now DNA was the new silver bullet in the detectives' arsenal. In June of that year, semen lifted from the five Oakland murder victims was sent for analysis. Those tests delivered exactly the outcome that investigators had expected. All of the women had been killed by the same man, and that man was Anthony McKnight.

It was a win for the law officers who'd believed all along in McKnight's guilt and also for the families of the victims, who were desperate for closure. But justice proved a long time coming in the McKnight case. For 19 long years, the matter dragged through the courts, going through continuance after continuance, delay after delay. During that time, McKnight made 46 court appearances, although seldom with the same attorney since his public defender was constantly changing. One thing remained constant, though. He continued to deny culpability. He also appeared to take joy at tormenting the families of his victims, scanning the courtroom to find them and laughing when they met his gaze.

The laughter finally dried up for Anthony McKnight in November 2008, when he was convicted on multiple counts of murder and sentenced to death. Justice may have taken its time, but in the end, the vicious killer got exactly what he deserved.

Joseph Miller

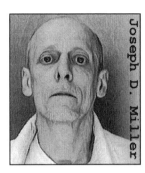

A killer was prowling the streets of Harrisburg, Pennsylvania, trawling for the easiest prey of all, women who were foolhardy enough to stick out a thumb and get into a car with a complete stranger.

The first victim to die at the hands of this ruthless predator was 18-year-old Selina Franklin who, along with a group of friends, accepted a ride from a man named Joey on May 16, 1987. That had seemed like a safe bet. Joseph Miller was known to the girls and often offered rides in the neighborhood. It was perhaps for that reason that Selina felt secure in remaining in the car after her friends had been dropped off. She was never seen alive again. Joseph Miller was, of course, questioned regarding Selina's disappearance, but he insisted that he'd dropped her off safely. Once his wife backed up his story, the police were forced to let the matter drop. Selina's body would be found four years later at a landfill in Swatara Township.

It is very likely that Stephanie McDuffey also felt secure in accepting a ride from a stranger. After all, the 23-year-old was eight months pregnant, and what kind of a monster would harm an expectant mother? A monster like Joseph Miller, as it turned out. Stephanie accepted that fateful ride on November 6, 1989. She was driven to the Swatara Township landfill where she was raped and beaten to death with an iron bar. Her body would be found years later, buried under a pile of roof shingles, weighted down with old tires.

Just two months later, on January 11, 1990, 25-year-old Jeannette Thomas left a bar in the Allison Hill area of Harrisburg, having accepted the offer of a ride from a man she'd just met. She was later found stabbed and beaten to death at the Swatara Township landfill, but at least, in this case, there was a suspect. Bar patrons told detectives that Jeanette had left with a man named William Kelly, and Kelly soon cracked under questioning and confessed to the crime. He was subsequently tried, convicted, and sentenced to 20 years in prison.

Did the police believe that Kelly was also the killer of Selina Franklin and Stephanie McDuffey? Did they believe that they'd taken a serial killer off the streets? Perhaps. But if they did believe that, they were wrong. On February 27, 1990, the body of Kathy Novena Shenck was found at a roadside dump in Perry County. Evidence suggested that she had been run over by a car, but this was no accident. Her killer had knocked her down and then backed up and driven over her again and again, crushing her under his wheels.

Thus far, Joseph Miller had murdered four women, his level of violence escalating with each crime. On June 30, 1992, he struck again, this time abducting a Harrisburg prostitute, driving her to a remote area near Wheatfield Township, and then sexually assaulting her and forcing her to perform oral sex. He then launched a savage attack on the woman, stabbing her more than 25 times in the head with a screwdriver before driving off, leaving her for dead.

But the woman wasn't dead. Miraculously she survived and staggered to a nearby house. Later, from her hospital bed, she provided Pennsylvania State troopers with a vital clue. She said that her attacker had stopped at an ATM after picking her up. Detectives then subpoenaed surveillance footage from the bank and had a clear picture of the man they were hunting. Joseph Miller could be seen in the foreground. In the background was his car, with the victim visible in the passenger seat.

Miller was arrested on August 6, 1992. On August 12, he led officers to the as yet undiscovered bodies of Selina Franklin and Stephanie McDuffey. He later confessed to four killings, including that of Jeannette Thomas, for which an innocent man was currently behind bars. William Kelly was later exonerated and released. It would emerge that Kelly suffered frequent blackouts due to his alcoholism and was often unable to recall what he may have done. He had believed for all these years that he had murdered Jeannette Thomas.

The real killer, Joseph Miller, would never be tried for the Thomas murder. He would, however, be convicted for the killings of Selina

Franklin and Stephanie McDuffey and sentenced to death. That sentence was later commuted to life imprisonment when a Dauphin County judge ruled that Miller was mentally handicapped.

Donald Murphy

Cheryl Harris wasn't in the habit of fraternizing with customers. But Don was a regular at the Detroit lounge where she worked as a waitress; he was always polite and friendly and he always asked for her by name. Plus, he was a generous tipper. And so, when he offered her a ride home on a freezing December night in 1980, she was happy to accept. That would turn out to be the worst mistake she ever made. Along the route, Don suddenly pulled to the side of a darkened road, drew a knife and held it to her throat.

Terrified, Cheryl grabbed for the door handle but couldn't work it open. At that moment, the interior of the car was suddenly flooded with light as another vehicle approached. Cheryl opened her mouth to scream, but any hope of rescue was quickly extinguished as Don pulled her down into the seat and buried her petite, 5-foot-1-inch frame under his bulk. That was when she got her teeth around his hand and bit down so hard that she could taste his blood in her mouth. But the bite only served to infuriate her attacker. He started beating her, then choking her, tightening his grip until she could feel herself slipping away. She was sure that she was dying.

Only, Cheryl didn't die. She awoke sometime later when the sky was beginning to lighten. She soon realized that she was in a moving vehicle, that she was naked, and that her wrists and ankles were tied with her own pantyhose. As consciousness gradually returned, she realized that she was in Don's car, driving who knows where. Wherever it was, though, it was taking a long time to get there. Lapsing in and out of consciousness, Cheryl at least had the presence of mind to play dead. After what felt like hours, the car finally came to a halt. Then she was dragged from the vehicle and dumped in a ditch. Moments later, she heard the car driving away.

Cheryl had no idea where she was. But over the next few hours, she somehow managed to find her way to a farmhouse, passing out again as she dragged herself onto the porch. Her next recollection was of being in an ambulance. Later, after being treated for her injuries, she was able to speak to detectives and provide the name of her attacker. Within hours, 36-year-old Donald Murphy, an ex-con with a history of violent attacks on women, was in custody. Cheryl Harris didn't know it yet, but she had just survived an encounter with a serial killer.

On December 15, 1980, the day that a Detroit PD tactical team took Donald Murphy into custody, the department had as many as fifteen unsolved homicides of women on its books. Two of those were resolved when Murphy admitted that he was the man who had beaten prostitute Cynthia Warren to death on October 23. It was also he who had stabbed and strangled Cecilia Knott, another streetwalker, on November 7. But Murphy wasn't stopping there. He soon confessed that he was responsible for raping, slashing, and strangling 24-year-old prostitute Jeanette Woods on April 18. He'd also committed two more murders, strangling 22-year-old Diane Burks on July 24, and stabbing and bludgeoning 26-year-old Betty Rembert on October 8.

Usually, the police would have been delighted to clear up five unsolved homicides in the course of a single interview. In this case, however, they were perplexed and just a little bit miffed. They already had a suspect in custody for the Woods, Burks, and Rembert murders. The man who had confessed to the killings was a popular local athlete named David Payton. Except that now, Payton wanted to recant and was making a lot of noise about the 84 hours of police grilling he'd been subjected to. According to him, his confession had been coerced. Now, with someone else admitting to the murders, the Detroit police department faced public embarrassment.

The matter was eventually resolved when the charges against Payton were dismissed in March 1981. Murphy, meanwhile, was charged with two counts of murder (Warren and Knott) and received concurrent 30-year prison terms. As for the other three murders, they remain technically unsolved to this day.

.

William "Cody" Neal

Born on October 7, 1955, in Fort Belvoir, Virginia, William Lee Neal grew up in a strict and religious home. His father was an Air Force officer who ran a tight ship and did not believe in sparing the rod. William, as the only son, was often the outlet for his frustration, especially since his sisters ganged up on him and made up stories to their father in order to get him punished. Neal Sr. also made a habit of taking his pre-teen son to dive bars, where he took pleasure in humiliating the boy in front of his drinking buddies.

When Neal was in his teens, he was seduced by an older, married woman, an encounter that appeared to awaken his sexuality. Thereafter, he became obsessed with sex, a fixation he'd carry with him into adulthood. By his twenties, he had turned his pursuit of women into a near full-time occupation. He would later boast that he'd seduced thousands of women in his lifetime. That is most likely an exaggeration, but Neal was certainly popular with the opposite sex. He was reasonably good-looking and had a glib line of talk and a talent for manipulation. He also conjured up an "outlaw" persona which women seemed to like. He was now calling himself "Cody Neal" or "Wild Bill Cody."

But like most sexually aggressive men, Neal was a misogynist at heart. He could be charming when he needed to be, but the real Cody Neal was a different creature altogether – a possessive, paranoid control freak with quick fists and a short temper. The four women he'd marry would all walk out on him due to the sadistic abuse they suffered. Others would not make it out of the relationship alive.

In June 1998, Cody Neal was living in Colorado with his long-term girlfriend, Rebecca Holberton. The couple had been together for two years, but the relationship was failing. The reasons were the same as they always were with Cody Neal – physical abuse and Neal's infidelity. Rebecca was also pushing for the repayment of $70,000 that Neal had borrowed from her over the course of their relationship. At the same time, Neal was also involved with a second woman, Candace Walters, to whom he owed an additional $6,000. She, too, was pressing him for payment and threatening to reveal their relationship to Holberton unless he paid up.

That, regrettably, was the wrong strategy to employ with a man like Cody Neal. Neal did not take kindly to threats. As he sat fretting over his predicament, his anger began pushing him in the direction of a horrific solution. In late June, he visited a local hardware store and bought several items, including rolls of plastic sheeting, duct tape and nylon rope. He also purchased a seven-and-a-half-pound splitting maul, a sinister-looking tool with a head that is half axe, half sledgehammer.

In early July, Rebecca arrived home at her apartment to be met at the door by a grinning Cody. He told her that he had a surprise for her and asked her to sit on the couch while he fetched it. Then, as Rebecca sat innocently waiting, he crept up behind her and swung the axe, burying the blade deep in her skull. Later, he wrapped the body in plastic and secured it with duct tape. Then, he stood it upright against a wall and started cleaning up the blood.

A couple of days later, Neal lured Candace Walters to his apartment, telling her that Rebecca was out of town and that he'd come into some money and could repay what he owed. Instead, he repaid Candace with the sharp end of the axe buried deep in her skull.

And still Neal wasn't done. The murders had stirred up his lust for blood. Three days after killing Candace, he brought two more women to the apartment. Angela Fite was another of Neal's lovers; Suzanne Scott was an acquaintance who he'd been trying to seduce. The women were treated to a true horror show as Neal overpowered them and tied them up. "Welcome to my mortuary," he announced as he unwrapped the bodies of Rebecca Holberton and Candace Walters and showed them to his terrified captives. He then picked up the maul and hacked Angela Fite to death, forcing Suzanne Scott to watch. Suzanne must have thought that she was next, but instead Neal raped and sodomized her before setting her free. He warned her not to go to the police but, of course, Suzanne did exactly that. Neal was arrested within hours of releasing her.

Cody Neal was convicted of three counts of first-degree murder in 1999. He was condemned to death, but the sentence was later commuted to life in prison. It is unlikely that he will ever be released.

Itzcoatl Ocampo

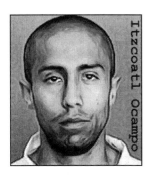

Someone was killing the homeless of Orange County, California. Already, three men were dead, brutally hacked to death by a knife-wielding attacker. The first to die was 53-year-old James McGillivray, who was stabbed to death in a delivery bay at the Placentia shopping center. That was on December 20, 2011, and the entire incident was captured on surveillance video. It showed a black-clad man, wearing a black beanie, attacking McGillivray as he slept and stabbing him to death.

Just over a week later, on December 28, there was another murder. The victim was 42-year-old Lloyd Middaugh, found stabbed to death in a dry riverbed in Orange County. The condition of the crime scene suggested that he, too, had been sleeping when he was attacked. And the knife wounds pointed to a weapon similar to the one used on James McGillivray.

And then, just two days later, there was a third murder, this time behind a Bank of America branch in Yorba Linda. The victim, 57-

year-old Paulus Smit, had been savagely stabbed and slashed, and surveillance footage from the bank showed a clear image of the killer. He was a young man, athletically built and dressed all in black, with a black beanie. An exact physical match, in other words, for the man who had killed James McGillivray. It was then that the authorities' worst fears were realized. There was a serial killer on the streets, one who had claimed three lives in the space of just ten days.

On January 13, 2012, 32-year-old Donald Hopkins was shopping at a CVS Pharmacy in Yorba Linda when a man entered the store screaming for help. Hopkins immediately dropped his shopping basket and rushed outside. The sight that greeted him was almost beyond belief. There, in broad daylight, in a busy shopping center, was a man stabbing another man, raining down blows on his helpless victim with a viciously curved blade.

"Hey, stop!" Hopkins shouted, at which the attacker, standing just 15 feet away, broke off the attack, glanced briefly at Hopkins and then sprinted across the parking lot.

Hopkins gave chase, simultaneously reaching in his pocket for his cellphone. Then he had to stop to punch in 911 and make the call, allowing the attacker to gain some distance on him. Minutes later, the police arrived, and Hopkins pointed them in the direction the attacker had fled. He was soon found hiding in a storage area and arrested.

By now, paramedics were on the scene and attending to the victim, a 64-year-old homeless man named John Barry. Unfortunately, his injuries were so severe that there was nothing they could do to save him. His attacker, meanwhile, had been taken to the local police precinct where he was identified as 23-year-old Itzcoatl Ocampo, a former US Marine who had served a tour of duty in Iraq. Ocampo's family was stunned at his arrest, saying that he'd previously volunteered for charities that helped the homeless but that his experiences in the military had changed him.

Ocampo was indicted on four counts of first-degree murder. But before he could go on trial, he was connected to another massacre, the brutal double homicide of a mother and son. Raquel Estrada, 53, and Juan Herrera, 34, had been stabbed to death in their Yorba Linda home on October 25, 2011, just over a month before Ocampo started his deadly campaign against the homeless. Raquel Estrada's younger son, Eder, (a former school friend of Ocampo) had originally been arrested for the double murder, but now DNA linked Ocampo to the crime. It was also determined that it was his 7-inch KA-BAR knife that had been used in the killings. The same weapon had taken the lives of the four homeless victims.

Itzcoatl Ocampo was indicted on six counts of first-degree murder. However, he would never stand trial. He died in prison in November 2013 after ingesting a lethal dose of an industrial cleaner. His death was ruled a suicide.

Michael Player

During the 1970s and 80s, Los Angeles, California, was a particularly dangerous place for a vagrant to eke out a living. With its pleasant year-round climate, the city was a magnet for homeless drifters, many of them congregating around the downtown district known as Skid Row. This made them easy targets for "mission-based" serial killers and L.A. had more than its fair share of those during that era – men like Vaughn Greenwood, Bobby Joe Maxwell, and "Koreatown Slasher" Joseph Danks; men like Norman Bernard and Michael Player.

On the morning of September 4, 1986, LAPD officers were called to the scene of a homicide at the corner of Venice Boulevard and Clarington Avenue in Culver City. The victim was 54-year-old Rudolfo Roque, and he had been killed by a single

.22-caliber bullet, fired into the back of his head at close range. Unlike the victims who would follow, Roque was not homeless. He was a visitor from San Diego, who appeared to have been killed during a holdup. Such crimes, unfortunately, are an aspect of life in any big city.

But at least, in this instance, there was a lead. As officers were processing the scene, a young African-American man stepped out of the gathered crowd and said that he had some information about the shooting. The man, who identified himself as Marcus Nisby, was taken to Pacific Division headquarters where he was questioned by detectives. But the information he gave was vague and contradictory, leading detectives to wonder if Nisby, himself, had been involved in the shooting. Still, they had nothing to link him to the murder, and so they let him go. That would turn out to be a mistake.

Over the next month, the Skid Row area experienced an unprecedented spate of shootings, many of them linked by ballistics to the same .22 that had killed Rudolfo Roque. The first to die was 66-year-old Ricky Stamps, gunned down in an alleyway on September 9. Four days later, there were two more shootings. Rojello Sirven was killed outright, while a second victim, 47-year-old Joseph Griffin, was rushed to hospital and received emergency surgery that failed to save him. He would eventually lose his fight for life on October 5.

And the carnage was only just getting started. Michael Singer, age 66, was executed by a .22 slug to the back of the head on September 20; David Towns was shot to death in his sleep three days later. September 30 brought two more murders, with victims Christopher Boyle and Leon Gaines shot dead in separate incidents. Then the killer took a week-long break before re-emerging on October 7 to gun down 23-year-old Chang Kang, a visitor from Texas. One day later, there was a tenth victim when 44-year-old Wayne Ellis was shot and killed in Athens Park. After that, inexplicably, the shootings stopped.

Investigators were puzzled by this sudden cessation. In their experience, a killer this prolific was very unlikely to stop of his own volition. That left only two possible explanations. Either the shooter been arrested on some other charge and was currently locked up somewhere, or he was dead. Perhaps some intended victim had got the drop on him.

Working this angle, detectives started checking the city's morgues, trying to find a recently deceased individual who matched their suspect. They knew, from the only man who had survived an encounter with the shooter, that he was African-American and in his mid-twenties. Soon they had a likely candidate, a 26-year-old man named Marcus Nisby who had died from a self-inflicted gunshot wound to the head.

The name "Nisby" immediately jangled with investigators. Marcus Nisby was the witness who had come forward after the first shooting. Checking into his background, detectives learned that his name wasn't Nisby at all. He was Michael Player, a habitual criminal with a record for theft, armed robbery, and parole violations.

So how had Player ended up in the morgue? Apparently, he'd checked into a Wilshire Boulevard hotel on October 10, paying in cash and signing the register as "Marcus Nisby." He'd then gone up to his room, lay down on the bed and shot himself.

Ballistic evidence would soon link Michael Player to the Skid Row shootings. The .22-caliber revolver he'd used to kill himself was the same weapon that had ended the lives of his ten victims. The case was officially closed in February 1987.

Darrell Rich

The state of California has more death row inmates than any other in the nation. This is not because California hands down more death sentences than other states, but rather because it has a particularly burdensome appeals process which condemned inmates exploit to delay their executions, often by decades. In California, a condemned person is more likely to die of old age than by lethal injection. Since the turn of the century, only six men have been executed in the state.

One of those who did feel the lethal sting of the needle was a serial killer named Darrell Rich, who was put to death in March of 2000. A Native American of Cherokee origin, Rich was convicted of the murders of three young women and an 11-year-old girl. And it is easy to see why a jury decided that he was eligible for the ultimate punishment. His crimes rank among the most heinous in American criminal history.

The first woman to fall victim to this predator was Annette Edwards, who disappeared from her home in Redding, California, in early July 1978. Her body was found three days later, tossed down an embankment along a remote road. She had been brutally raped and then beaten to death with a rock, the blows delivered with such force that both of her eye sockets had collapsed.

About a month later, with the police no closer to identifying the killer of Annette Edwards, two more Redding women went missing within the space of a couple of days. The first of those was 17-year-old Patricia Moore, who disappeared from a motel in early August; the second was Linda Slavik, aged 26, who vanished from a bar in Chico, California, just days later. Their bodies would be found two weeks later at a dump in Igo. Before that discovery, there was one more murder, perhaps the most heartrending of all.

On the afternoon of August 13, 1978, 11-year-old Annette Selix left her home in Cottonwood and walked to a nearby market to buy groceries. She promptly disappeared, sparking a police search that would be tragically resolved the following morning. Annette's broken body was found at the foot of a bridge in Shasta County. An autopsy would determine that she was still alive when she was tossed from the 105-foot precipice to be smashed on the rocks below. She'd lived just long enough to curl herself into a fetal position. The medical examiner also determined that she had been raped, sodomized, and forced to perform oral copulation. Her killer had also inflicted deep bite marks on her thighs.

This horrific murder left the police doubly determined to catch the man responsible. But the investigation was going nowhere until August 20, when there was a surprise break in the case. A man called the police and reported that he had found two bodies at the Igo dump.

That man was Darrell Rich and the bodies were those of murder victims, Patricia Moore and Linda Slavik. Moore, like earlier victim Annette Edwards, had been clubbed to death with a rock; Slavik had been shot, with the killer apparently forcing the gun barrel into her mouth before pulling the trigger. Both women had been savagely raped, and the police were beginning to form an idea as to who was responsible.

From the very start, investigators had been suspicious of Rich's story. He claimed that he'd discovered the bodies by chance while riding his motorcycle around the dump. But his motorcycle was a street bike, which would have struggled with the terrain, and there were also no tire tracks where he claimed to have ridden. Then the police learned something else about Rich. He had previously done handyman work for Annette Selix's mother. That put him in proximity of yet another of the murder victims.

Rich, though, was giving nothing away. He staunchly denied involvement in the murders and maintained that stance even after he failed a polygraph. With no way of proving otherwise, the police were forced to let him go. He might well have gotten away with murder, had he been able to keep his mouth shut.

But like most serial killers, Rich enjoyed bragging about his misdeeds. Hanging out at the Oarlock Bar in Redding, he liked to boast about the murders, even doing falsetto-voiced impressions of how his victims begged for their lives in their final moments. Once reports of these macabre parodies got back to investigators, Rich was taken into custody. This time, he broke under interrogation and confessed, adding five particularly brutal rapes to his long rap sheet.

Darrell Rich was tried, convicted and sentenced to death. He was executed by lethal injection on March 15, 2000.

Ramon Rogers

Beatrice Toronczak's mother was worried about her. Beatrice had only recently moved to San Diego from her native Poland, and now she was missing. And her former boyfriend, the father of her 6-year-old son, was no help at all. He said that Beatrice had left their shared apartment three weeks earlier and had not returned. He also refused to file a missing person report with the police. Eventually, Mrs. Toronczak became so frustrated with his stonewalling that she contacted a friend in America and asked her to go to the police. That was on March 6, 1996.

The report regarding Beatrice Toronczak's disappearance landed on the desk of San Diego police detective Richard Carlson. The officer then phoned Beatrice's ex, a bit-part actor named Ramon Jay Rogers, and asked when last he'd seen the 32-year-old. Rogers said that it was about ten days ago and then said that he was busy and hung up the phone. That immediately roused the detective's suspicions.

About three hours later, Detective Carlson arrived at Rogers's apartment with a team of uniformed officers, ready to carry out a search. Rogers wasn't home, and so the searchers moved down to the basement. According to Beatrice's mother, Rogers had often threatened to lock Beatrice inside a storage unit that he kept down there.

But before they were able to open the unit, Rogers showed up, full of righteous indignation, and refused them access. Carlson, concerned that the young woman might be locked inside, decided to enter anyway. He ordered his team to break the lock. They'd barely entered when they found a hammer, a saw, and a butcher knife, all of them bloodstained. Further investigation uncovered severed fingers and parts of a jawbone wrapped in a plastic bag. These were later determined to belong to Beatrice Toronczak. As the police were soon to discover, she was not the only one of Rogers's close associates to suddenly disappear.

Ron Stadt had been Rogers's best friend, although the friendship had soured after Stadt discovered that Rogers was seeing his estranged wife, Debra, behind his back. On June 24, 1993, Rogers and Stadt became involved in a heated conversation over the telephone. Stadt was at work at the time, but after hanging up, he told colleagues that he was going to Rogers's apartment to pick up some jewelry that his wife had left there. That was the last time they saw him. Rogers, when questioned by police, said that Stadt had picked up the jewelry and then left. He'd later made a number of potentially incriminating statements to friends, saying that Ron was "mountain lion food" and that he would never bother Debra again. Ron Stadt's body has never been found.

Rogers was also a suspect in the murder of his former girlfriend, Rose Albano. This time, it was Rogers, himself, who had filed the missing person report, calling it in on December 23, 1994. He told the police that he'd last seen Rose on December 12 and that he was concerned about her because she was pregnant and had been carrying a large sum of cash. Rose Albano's partial remains were found on December 29, 1993, stashed in a trash bag and discarded in a mountainous area. The location was just a mile from Rogers's sister's home, a location he'd recently visited. Further investigation revealed that Albano had recently drawn $4,600 from her retirement fund. That money was now missing. Shortly after her disappearance, Rogers spent nearly $4,000 on new tires and an engine overhaul for his truck. He also told friends that Rose had been pressuring him to marry her but that he'd wanted to end the relationship because he didn't want to take responsibility for her two children.

At the time of Rose Albano's death, the authorities had felt that there was insufficient evidence to file charges against Rogers. Now, they obtained indictments for three counts of first-degree murder. At trial, the defense tried to have the Toronczak evidence thrown out, saying that it was obtained during an illegal search. However, the police are allowed to enter without a warrant if they suspect that someone is in imminent danger. Since that was clearly the case here, the objection was overruled.

Ramon Rogers was convicted on two counts of first-degree murder and one of second-degree murder. He was sentenced to death and currently awaits execution. He remains a suspect in at least two other murders, both of them involving dismemberment.

Michael Ronning

Monday, January 3, 1985, was an ordinary day in the life of Darrell Meredith. He got up early, took a shower and had coffee with his girlfriend, Diana Hanley. At around 7:20, he set off for work at a house he was building in Jonesboro, Arkansas. Diana kissed him goodbye at the door wearing a red robe he'd bought her for Christmas. At the job site, Meredith was miffed to find that one of the men he'd recently hired hadn't shown up for work. That put the whole team under added pressure.

But problems with errant employees would soon be the least of Darrell Meredith's problems. When he got home that night, he found Diana gone. Her car was in the drive and her coat, purse, and keys were inside the house, but of Diana, herself, there was no sign. Also, a strongbox that had contained several hundred dollars in cash had been broken into. Also missing was a large hunting knife. Meredith immediately called the police.

An early break in the case came when investigators learned that a beat-up, cream-colored Plymouth had been seen parked in the drive of the house that morning. Meredith knew that car. It belonged to Michael Haroldson, the recently hired construction worker who had failed to show up for work that day. Further investigation revealed that Haroldson was actually Michael Ronning, an ex-con currently wanted on burglary charges in Michigan. A call was then placed to the Randolph County Sheriff's department to pick up Ronning, who was living with his family in Pocahontas. He was taken into custody in the early hours of January 7.

Under interrogation, Ronning initially denied knowing anything about Diana Hanley's whereabouts. But his denials were a lot more difficult to support after her body was found in dense brush on January 19. She was still in the red robe she'd been wearing on the morning of her disappearance, but now it was disarranged and bloodstained. The young woman's throat had been savagely cut, and she had also suffered three potentially fatal stab wounds, inflicted with a large knife. Bruises and abrasions to the upper thighs suggested that she had been raped although the medical examiner couldn't say for sure, due to advanced decomposition. Michael Ronning was ultimately convicted of her murder and sentenced to life in prison.

And the story might well have ended there – just another tragic tale of a heartless killer and an innocent and defenseless victim. But then, in 2002, NBC's Dateline did a program on the murder, and Ronning built up a rapport with producer Shane Bishop. During the course of their conversations, Ronning admitted to Bishop that he was responsible for six more murders – in Michigan, Texas, and Florida. He'd be willing to talk to investigators in those states, but only if he had guarantees that the death penalty was off the table. Those assurances, regrettably, were not forthcoming, even after Bishop wrote directly to Governors Rick Perry and Jeb Bush and asked for their intervention.

But who are the six victims that Michael Ronning was referring to? The Michigan cases appear to reference a trio of homicides committed in the Battle Creek area between 1982 and 1983, while Ronning was living in the area. The victims were all young women, stabbed to death, their bodies hidden in dense woodland. Ronning did, in fact, speak to Michigan investigators, but they felt he was being untruthful and sent him back to Arkansas without filing charges.

The Texas authorities, meanwhile, would like to talk to Ronning about the murder of 20-year-old Annette Melia, who disappeared near Bedford in 1982 and was found in 1985. They also believe that Ronning is responsible for the death of Melissa Jackson. The 16-year-old's body was found in the woods near Bedford in 1986. Again, these homicides coincided with Ronning's presence in the area and bear his unique signature.

But perhaps the most compelling case to be connected to Ronning is that of a Jane Doe found in the Ocala National Forest near Lake Dorr, Florida on April 18, 1984. Ronning and his wife, Victoria, had been living in a mobile home in nearby Umatilla at the time. He had a good job there, working construction in Seminole County. Then one day in April, he suddenly told Victoria that they had to leave.

So why would Ronning walk out so abruptly on a stable job and a steady income? Given his history, there can only be one reason. Lake County detectives firmly believe that Ronning is the man responsible for the Ocala Forest murder. Without assurances regarding the death penalty, he is not prepared to discuss the matter.

Gary Sampson

Hitchhiking is a perilous undertaking, fraught with danger for both the driver offering the ride and the hitcher accepting it. You're getting into a car with a complete stranger, putting your trust in his or her goodwill. And sometimes that trust is misplaced, as anyone who accepted a ride from Pee Wee Gaskins or Ed Kemper found out; as anyone who picked up Otis Toole or Aileen Wournos soon realized.

Another hitchhiking serial killer, lesser known than those mentioned above, was Gary Lee Sampson. Born in Weymouth, Massachusetts, on September 29, 1959, Sampson grew to be a bright child although afflicted by dyslexia, which caused him to struggle in formal education. He eventually dropped out of school in the 9th grade. By then, he already had an extensive juvenile record for theft and burglary. He barely broke stride before transitioning into the adult prison system. Between 1976 and 2001, he was in and out of correctional facilities on various offenses, although he still found time during that period to marry and divorce five times and to father three children.

Sampson was an unconventional criminal who made use of elaborate disguises while carrying out his favorite kind of felony, bank heists. Often, he dressed as a woman, a skill he'd learned from a transvestite lover. But his disguise would fail him during a five-robbery spree in North Carolina in 2001. He was picked up on surveillance cameras and identified, resulting in a warrant being issued for his arrest.

Fearful that he might be killed in a confrontation with the police, Sampson fled back to his home state of Massachusetts. From there, he phoned the FBI and offered to surrender. Unfortunately, the call was accidentally disconnected while Sampson was on the line, and he failed to call back. That simple error would have dire consequences. A day later, he hit the road and stuck out his thumb. Gary Sampson was about to embark on a murder spree.

Sixty-nine-year-old Philip McCloskey was on his way to visit a friend in Weymouth, Massachusetts, when he spotted Sampson at the roadside and stopped to give him a ride. That kindness would come at a heavy cost. The elderly man was forced at knifepoint to drive to some woods near Taunton. There Sampson pulled him from the car, dragged him up a hill, stabbed him 24 times, and watched him bleed to death. He then drove away in McCloskey's car, although he later abandoned it.

The following day, Sampson was hitchhiking in the South Shore area when 19-year-old college student Jonathan Rizzo stopped to pick him up. Sampson then forced Rizzo to drive to a wooded area near Abington, where the teenager was tied to a tree and stabbed multiple times. Sampson then left in Rizzo's Volkswagen Jetta, heading for New Hampshire. There, he broke into an empty home in the town of Meredith, staying the night. When 59-year-old maintenance man, Robert Whitney, showed up to work on the house the next morning, Sampson overpowered him and strangled him to death. He then made breakfast and drank some beer before heading out again.

Gary Sampson would attempt one more carjacking, this time in Vermont. However, his intended victim escaped, and Sampson then decided to give himself up. After breaking into a house, he called the police and gave them his location. He was there, meekly waiting to surrender, when they arrived. Led away in cuffs, he was subsequently extradited to Massachusetts to await trial.

Given that the state of Massachusetts does not have the death penalty, Sampson probably figured that he was safe from execution. That is most likely why he spoke so freely about his crimes, describing the three murders he'd committed in graphic detail. But Sampson had miscalculated. Two of the three murders had occurred during the commission of a carjacking. And since carjacking is a federal offense, his trial would be heard before a federal judge in Boston. That meant, of course, that Sampson was eligible for capital punishment. And the prosecutor made no bones about his intentions. He was going to see to it that Gary Sampson got the death penalty.

Faced with this prospect, Sampson nonetheless decided to leave his confession on the record and to plead guilty at his December

2003 trial. Perhaps he thought that his co-operation would save him. It didn't. Found guilty on three counts of murder, he was sentenced to death. He currently awaits execution in New Hampshire.

Della Sorenson

The village of Dannebrog is a tiny hamlet in central Nebraska, home to just over 300 people. Founded by immigrants from Denmark in 1871, it retains a strong Danish influence to this day. Back in the early 1900s, when our story takes place, the population was made up almost exclusively of expatriate Danes.

One of the families living in Dannebrog at that time was the Weldmans – Joseph, his wife Della, and their infant daughter, Minnie. Joseph's elderly mother also lived in the household, although Della did not particularly like the old woman. In fact, she disliked her husband's family in general, particularly her sister-in-law, Ingrid Cooper, who she claimed had "blackened her name" around the village.

In July 1918, Ingrid Cooper arrived at the Weldman household for a visit, bringing her infant daughter with her. Della, who appears to have been adept at hiding her true feelings, greeted her sister-in-law with open arms. She also fussed and flapped over the babe. Deep inside, though, she was seething. Ingrid had bad-mouthed her, and she was intent on revenge. Tragically, it was little Viola who paid the price. On the first morning of the visit, Della slipped strychnine into the child's porridge, and Viola died within hours. Later, Della would say that her niece's death left her with "a feeling of elation."

The murder of Viola Cooper would set a deadly precedent, with Della Weldman now relying on her vial of poison to right every perceived wrong. In September 1920, she decided to get rid of her husband who'd had the temerity to raise his voice to her. Joseph Weldman ate a bowl of his favorite broth and died in agony soon after. He was followed to the grave by his mother. The old woman had been left in Della's care, but a dash of strychnine ushered her off into the afterlife and relieved Della of her burden. Soon after, there was another tragedy in the Weldman household. Della's daughter Minnie suddenly became ill. She died within days, despite her mother's tender nursing.

Minnie's death left Della all alone in the world, but she would not remain so for long. Within four months, she was marching down the aisle with Emmanuel Sorenson.

Over the next two years, Della Sorenson appears to have kept her murderous instincts in check. But a visit from her former sister-in-law in August seems to have got her riled up again. Despite having murdered Ingrid Cooper's first-born child, Della still harbored a grudge. Ingrid had another child now, a sweet-natured four-month-old named Clifford. Tragically, Clifford did not survive the visit. He died after Della put strychnine in his milk. She would later try to poison another of the Cooper children, although, thankfully, this child survived.

Della Sorenson had embarked on her poisoning spree out of her lust for revenge over petty grievances. But, like so many serial killers before her, she had become addicted to the act of murder. Now, with no other victims readily available, she turned her attention to her own family. In February 1923, she murdered one-year-old Ruth Brock, the daughter of a relative. "I felt sorry for the poor child," she'd later claim, "because its mother did not care for it."

That excuse would not have held up with her next victim, however. On February 19, 1924, Della's own baby daughter, Delia, was found dead. Then Della tried to poison her second husband. He survived, but by now the authorities were beginning to wonder. So many unexplained deaths in one family. Could it really be coincidence?

Despite those suspicions, Sorenson would remain at large for another year. During that time, she would attempt two more murders. Two neighborhood children were given strychnine-laced cookies and barely survived. When inquiries led the police to her door, Della admitted poisoning the children but maintained that she was justified because "their father stole a bottle of wine from me and I wanted to get even with him."

Della Sorenson was taken into custody on April 19, 1925, and soon confessed to seven murders. "I like attending funerals," she told her interrogators. "I'm only happy when someone is dying." Statements like this convinced the authorities that Sorenson was not dealing from a full deck. She was therefore sent to a mental hospital where doctors examined her and declared that she was schizophrenic. She would never stand trial for her crimes, instead seeing out her days at the state asylum, where she died on June 24, 1941.

Charles Stevens

California's intricate freeway system has been a seemingly irresistible magnet for serial killers over the years. During the 1970s and '80s, a trio of particularly brutal slayers – Patrick Kearney, William Bonin, and Randy Kraft – used these roads as their hunting ground, claiming over 100 victims between them. The exceptionally cruel duo of Lawrence Bittaker and Roy Norris also used the freeways, trawling for victims in a specially purposed van they dubbed "Murder Mack." And then there was Mack Ray Edwards, a Caltrans worker and child killer, who supposedly buried some of his victims under the Ventura Freeway.

Charles Arnett Stevens is not as infamous as any of the aforementioned killers. Yet, over a three-month period in 1989, the so-called "Recreational Killer" held the citizens of Oakland, California, in a grip of fear, afraid to drive their vehicles along the I-580, the killer's preferred hunting ground.

It started on the morning of April 3, 1989, when 29-year-old Leslie Ann Noyer was gunned down while walking along a suburban

Oakland street near the I-580. The young woman was hit three times in the face by high-powered bullets, later determined to have been fired from a .357-caliber handgun. There was no apparent motive – no robbery, no sexual assault. Neither was there anyone who might want to harm Leslie Ann, according to her family. So why had she been shot? The police didn't know, and that concerned them.

And they were right to be worried. Just a few weeks later, officers were called to the scene of an auto wreck on I-580 and discovered the body of 36-year-old Lori Anne Rochon. But the victim had not died in the crash; she had been shot to death. Ballistics would confirm that the murder weapon was the same gun that had killed Leslie Ann Noyer. There was a serial shooter on the loose.

Over the next two months, the "Recreational Killer" would carry out six more attacks. Karen Alice Anderson, Janell Lee, Julia Peters, Paul Fenn, and Upendra de Silva were all fired upon as they drove along the freeway. All escaped, some unharmed, others with minor injuries. Laquann Sloan was not so lucky. The 16-year-old was gunned down on an Oakland street in a shooting that was a near copy of the Noyer murder.

With the city by now in uproar and the police on high alert, you'd have thought that the killer would lie low for a while. But that is to misunderstand the motivations of psychopaths. They thrive on danger, often taking risks that ordinary people would consider outrageous. Charles Stevens was no different. On the night of Thursday, July 27, 1989, he loaded up his .357, got into his car and went trawling his favorite stretch of freeway again.

Twenty-four-year-old Rodney Stokes was also driving the I-580 that night, heading into Oakland, when a car pulled up alongside him. Stokes didn't see the weapon until the driver of the other vehicle started firing. Then he stood on the brakes and the other vehicle sped past. Miraculously, he had not been hit.

And then Rodney Stokes did an incredibly brave thing. Rather than pulling to the side of the road, as most would have done, he turned off his headlights and continued tailing the shooter, watching in horror as he fired at another car, as that car drifted off the road and came to a stop against the guard rail. Stokes pulled over, too, but he kept an eye on the shooter's vehicle, saw it exit the freeway and then park on the opposite on-ramp, apparently to watch the results of the carnage he'd wrought. He was still there when the police arrived, and Stokes pointed him out. Charles Stevens was arrested at the scene. The murder weapon, a .357-caliber Desert Eagle handgun, was found in his possession.

The latest victim of the killing spree, 28-year-old Raymond August, was dead before the paramedics arrived. His killer, Stevens, was taken to police headquarters where he arrogantly denied any involvement in the shootings. Not that the police required his confession. They had the murder weapon and an eyewitness statement. They also had a collection of newspaper clippings about the murders, pinned to a wall in Charles Stevens's house. When a friend of Stevens came forward to testify that he'd been in the car when Leslie Ann Noyer was shot, the case was made.

Charles Stevens was convicted on four counts of first-degree murder and sentenced to death. He has since been linked by DNA to another homicide, the April 1989 stabbing of 26-year-old Brenda Belvins.

Charles Terry

Have you heard about the Boston Strangler? That was the question posed by the Rolling Stones in their 1969 hit, Midnight Rambler. And, of course, most of us can answer, yes. It is, after all, one of the most infamous serial murder cases of all time. Albert DeSalvo took the fall and has since been linked by DNA to one of the murders, but DeSalvo was never charged. In fact, many criminologists believe that the Strangler was not one man but several, working independently of each other. One of the names that is frequently mentioned in connection with the case is Charles Terry.

Terry was born on May 26, 1930, in Waterville, Maine. He was an apparently happy child until the age of four, when he almost drowned in Messalonskee Lake during a family picnic. Thereafter, his parents began noticing subtle changes to his personality. He became more introverted and seemed reluctant to interact with his siblings or with other children.

Those personality traits would stay with Charles during his school years. Classmates described him as a loner and a misfit who was quick to anger. In 1947, he dropped out in the 10th grade and joined the Marines, serving until 1949, when his anti-social personality again got the best of him. While absent without leave, he stole a car and ended up being dishonorably discharged from the Corps.

Terry's first serious brush with the civilian authorities came in 1951 when he was a suspect in the murder of 24-year-old Shirley Coolen. Coolen was found in a flower garden in Brunswick, Maine, on May 26, 1951, strangled to death, with a scarf knotted around her neck. No charges were brought due to lack of evidence, but Terry was soon in trouble again when he was convicted of rape and sentenced to eight years at the Maine State Prison. There, he proved to be a troublesome inmate, causing disturbances and destroying property. He was also unpopular with other convicts, although most gave him a wide berth. Terry stood 6-foot-5 by now; he was tough and he had anger issues.

Released from prison in 1958, Terry was back inside within a year after he attacked a woman, fracturing her jaw in two places. A psychological exam during this incarceration diagnosed him as a sexual sadist but that did not prevent his parole. Free again, he married divorcee Theresa LaRochelle, beginning an on-again-off-again relationship. Theresa divorced him in 1961, while he was back in Maine State Prison on another sexual assault charge. However, the couple reconciled after his release and later had a son together.

Over the years that followed, Terry worked at a number of occupations, seldom remaining in a job for long due to his apparent inability to take direction. He lived in several locations, including New Orleans, Boston, and New York City. It was in New York that he would finally commit the atrocity that took him out of circulation for good.

On May 30, 1963, police were called to the scene of a savage murder in a Manhattan hotel room. The victim was 62-year-old Zenovia Clegg, and she had been brutally beaten, sexually assaulted with a liquor bottle and strangled with a scarf. There was little doubt as to the identity of the killer. Clegg had signed into the hotel with a man who was known to hotel staff. Charles Terry was tracked a week later to a Greenwich Village bar and arrested on the spot. He made no effort to deny that he'd killed Clegg. According the him, he'd been justified since she had enraged him by mocking his inability to perform sexually.

Unfortunately for Terry, the jury held a somewhat different view on the issue. Convicted of murder, he was sentenced to death, although the sentence was later commuted to life in prison. While serving that sentence, he was linked again to the Coolen murder and to another, the June 1958 slaying of 29-year-old Patricia Wing.

Wing's body had been found in a remote wooded area in Fairfield, raped, strangled and beaten to death. Her boyfriend, Everett Savage Jr., was initially charged but later acquitted. The case remained unsolved until investigators found a link to the man who had actually committed the crime – Charles Terry.

Charles Terry would never be charged with the Coolen and Wing murders. He died of lung cancer at Attica Correctional Facility in 1981. Since his death, he has been the subject of two books linking him to the Boston Strangler murders. NYPD detective, Thomas Cavanagh, the man who arrested him for the Clegg murder, was also a firm believer that Terry committed some of the infamous Boston slayings.

Daniel Troyer

On the morning of July 18, 1985, police in Salt Lake City, Utah, were called to the Logan Avenue residence of 83-year-old Drucilla Ovard. The elderly woman had been found lying naked on her bathroom floor, beaten and strangled to death. The police suspected a sexual motive and were somewhat surprised when the autopsy revealed that Mrs. Ovard had not been raped. However, detectives did find semen stains on a towel, evidence that the killer had masturbated over his victim's body. The towel was bagged as evidence, of course, but in those pre-DNA days, it was of limited use.

Two weeks after the murder, Salt Lake City PD received a call about a break-in at the residence of 70-year-old Carol Nelson. Mrs. Nelson was thankfully not at home, but a neighbor had spotted a man climbing through a window and had called the police. The would-be burglar was still inside the house when officers arrived and took him into custody. He was identified as 30-year-old Daniel Troyer.

Checking into Troyer's background, detectives soon discovered that he was currently on parole for an attack on a 71-year-old quadriplegic woman in 1978. Troyer was also nursing a broken hand, and the officers wondered if he might have sustained the injury while punching murder victim Drucilla Ovard during an attack so vicious that it had left the elderly woman with broken ribs. They put this theory to Troyer, but he denied having anything to do with the Ovard murder. With no evidence to say otherwise, the police were forced to let it drop. Troyer was eventually convicted of the Nelson burglary and was sent to prison for 15 years. He was paroled after just three.

On August 17, 1988, two weeks after Daniel Troyer walked free from prison, there was another brutal murder in Salt Lake City. The victim this time was 88-year-old Ethel Luckau, found strangled to death in her bed. One vital clue at the scene immediately led investigators to consider Troyer a suspect, a semen-stained towel. Then, as they looked into Troyer's movements, the case got even stronger. Troyer was living at a halfway house at the time, but on the day of the murder, he'd gone to apply for work at a barber college. The college was just three doors away from Mrs. Luckau's home.

It looked like a slam dunk case, but prosecutors were left reeling after a finicky judge suppressed their most crucial evidence. A statement from Troyer's sister that he had asked her to provide him with an alibi, was disallowed. So too was the testimony of two jailhouse snitches who claimed that Troyer had boasted to them about the murder. Most crucially, the judge blocked evidence that Troyer's DNA matched the semen found on the towel. This left prosecution with a mountain to climb, and it was no surprise when the charges against Troyer were dropped. It would be twelve more years before Salt Lake County prosecutors were eventually able to bring him to book.

As with many killers who escaped justice in the 1970s and '80s, it was technology that eventually caught up with Daniel Troyer. By 1997, DNA technology was sufficiently advanced to link Troyer to Drucilla Ovard's murder and allow charges to be filed. At the same time, prosecutors appealed the suppression of the DNA evidence in the Luckau case and obtained a ruling in their favor from the Utah Supreme Court. Daniel Troyer was ultimately convicted of two counts of murder and sentenced to consecutive life terms.

But are the murders of Drucilla Ovard and Ethel Luckau the only ones for which Troyer is responsible? Investigators in Salt Lake City think not. Troyer has frequently boasted to fellow inmates that elderly women are "easy targets" and has claimed involvement in thirteen murders.

At least two of those can be positively linked to Daniel Troyer. Thelma Lillian Blodgett, 69, was murdered in her South Salt Lake home on July 11, 1985, one week before Drucilla Ovard was killed. Lucille Westerman, 73, was a neighbor of Ethel Luckau who died under suspicious circumstances on August 23, 1988, six days after the Luckau murder. As for the other murders, they may well have gone unnoticed. Troyer often suffocated his victims to avoid leaving strangulation marks. He also arranged the murder scenes so that there was no evidence of a struggle.

Richard Valenti

On May 23, 1973, the concerned parents of two teenaged girls went to the police in Charleston, South Carolina and reported their daughters missing. Sherri Jan Clark, 15, and Alexis Ann Latimer, 14, had gone that morning to a house owned by Alexis's parents at Folly Beach. When they'd failed to return, their parents had gone looking for them. Finding no trace of the girls, they'd gone to the police.

A search was launched for Sherri and Alexis that night, continuing for several days but finding nothing. Months passed with no trace of them. Then, on September 27, a young naval cadet escaped an attempted abduction in the same area. Regrettably, she did not report the incident to the police, only to Navy officers who did nothing about it.

On February 12, 1974, a terrified teenager was found tied to a tree behind a shopping center in Folly Beach. According to the girl, she had been abducted at gunpoint by a tall, dark-haired man who had forced her to submit to being tied up. She had feared that she

might be raped or even killed, but the man had simply tied her up
and left her there.

That bizarre incident was followed by a more serious one, just
over a week later, on February 21. That was when another
teenaged girl went missing. Sixteen-year-old Mary Bunch had last
been seen walking along the beach by friends. Now she was gone,
and a massive search by police found no trace of her. Mary had still
not been found by mid-April, when another young woman
reported that a man had tried to abduct her at gunpoint. The
description given by the woman matched that of the man who had
tied the teenager to the tree several weeks earlier. With three
young girls missing from the area, and several attempted
abductions, the police were beginning to fear that they might have
a serial killer on their streets.

On April 12, the day after the latest abduction attempt, a police
officer was driving along a remote stretch of beach when he heard
screams. Tracking the sound to an isolated cottage, he entered and
discovered three teenaged girls, bound and gagged. Fortunately,
one of the girls had managed to loosen her gag and cry out.
Rescued from their ordeal, the girls told a story that was by now
familiar to the police. They had been abducted by a dark-haired
man with a gun. But for their screams, they probably would have
ended up dead.

Over the next few days, a sketch of the suspect was circulated in
the local press. That prompted several calls from the public, one of
which was of particular interest. A man reported that he'd been
walking his dog along a stretch of beach when the animal had

begun pawing at the sand in a particular spot. The location was close to the cottage from which the three girls had just been rescued.

Search teams were quickly dispatched to the area. They'd barely begun their exploration when they made a tragic discovery. The body of Mary Bunch was recovered from a shallow grave. She had been bound hand and foot with rope, and marks around her neck suggested ligature strangulation. The rope that had been used matched that from the other crime scenes.

By now, the South Carolina State Police had been called into the investigation. And they were about to get a big break in the case. The naval cadet who had escaped the abductor eight months earlier, finally came forward and identified her attacker. He was a fellow sailor, 32-year-old Richard Raymond Valenti. Brought in for questioning, Valenti soon cracked and admitted to three counts of murder and several counts of kidnapping and assault. He later led the police to the bodies of Sherri Clark and Alexis Latimer who had been buried just a short distance from Mary Bunch.

Explaining his motive for the murders, Valenti said that he could only achieve sexual arousal by seeing a woman "tied up and helpless." His ultimate fantasy was to see a woman with a noose around her neck. This was how his three victims had died. He'd hung them from an overhead pipe in the shower recess and watched as they slowly asphyxiated.

Richard Valenti went on trial in July 1974 with the prosecution determined to see him executed. The judge, however, decided that there were mitigating circumstances and sentenced the three-time killer to two life terms instead. Valenti has been eligible for parole since 1984. In 2014, he was turned down for the 18th time.

Billy Ray Waldon

Abandoned by his mother when he was just five years old, Billy Ray Waldon was raised by his maternal grandmother in Tahlequah, Oklahoma. He grew to be a handsome and intelligent young man, one who excelled at school and later reached the rank of first petty officer in the US Navy. After receiving an honorable discharge from the service in January 1985, he returned to his childhood home. Neighbors remember him as quiet, considerate and intelligent, with a deep fascination in his Cherokee heritage. His other interest was less conventional. He spent so much time talking about a cure for AIDS that friends and neighbors thought he might be suffering from the disease.

If Billy Ray had one defining relationship in his life, it was with his grandmother. He idolized the woman and was hit hard by her death in 1985. This, however, was no conventional grief response. Billy appeared to have undergone a personality shift. The once quiet, unassuming man was suddenly beset by a barely concealed rage. In the fall of 1985, that rage would bubble over into a deadly campaign of terror that would leave four people dead and at least eight injured.

Billy Waldon had never committed so much as a misdemeanor in his life, until the morning of October 10, 1985, when he walked up to an elderly man outside a Tulsa grocery store, drew a gun, and opened fire without provocation. That victim would survive and so too would 20-year-old Cynthia Bellinger, who was shot outside her parents' Tulsa home on November 15. Cynthia suffered no more than a flesh wound, but the next victim would not be so lucky. Annabelle Richmond, age 54, was shot and killed outside her apartment on November 17, four .25-caliber bullets ending her life.

With the police now alerted to the shooter in Tulsa, Waldon decamped for nearby Broken Arrow, where he shot and wounded two men in a botched holdup on November 23. He then fled west, heading for San Diego, a city he knew well from his Navy days. Within just a couple of weeks, he had unleashed a one-man crime spree, committing three rapes, five armed robberies, and a series of burglaries.

Waldon would soon graduate to murder. On December 7, he shot and killed 42-year-old Dawn Ellerman while burglarizing her home. He then started a fire, fleeing the scene as the blaze took hold. Thirteen-year-old Erin Ellerman arrived home from a babysitting job to find her house in flames. She died in a futile attempt to save her mother's life.

Two weeks later, on December 20, Waldon approached a woman in a San Diego parking lot and demanded money at gunpoint.

Rather than comply, the woman started to scream, forcing Waldon to flee. His escape route took him across a yard where 56-year-old Charles Wells and 36-year-old John Copeland were working on a car. Waldon demanded the keys but became frustrated when Wells tried to explain that the car was not drivable. He opened fire, cutting both men down in a hail of bullets. Copeland would survive. Wells would not.

A massive manhunt was now underway, involving 150 San Diego police officers. Yet Waldon somehow managed to avoid capture. Then, by chance, officers found an abandoned car containing various stolen items, including a computer that was traced to murder victim Dawn Ellerman. Also inside the vehicle was a military passport belonging to Billy Ray Waldon.

The pieces started to fall into place quite quickly after that. Waldon's last known address was in Tulsa, and when the San Diego police checked with their colleagues there, they learned about the series of unsolved shootings. Ballistics soon stitched the two crime sprees together, and a federal warrant was issued, charging Waldon with unlawful flight, murder, attempted murder, robbery, burglary, rape, and arson. On April 23, 1986, his name was added to the FBI's "Most Wanted" list.

But where was the fugitive? In Mexico, if the location of his latest stolen vehicle was anything to go by. It was found abandoned on a Tijuana street on January 27.

Waldon might well have escaped US justice had he remained south of the border. But he didn't. On June 16, he was pulled over by San Diego officers in a routine traffic stop. Asked for his name, he said that it was "Steven Midas." Fortunately, one of the cops remembered his face from a wanted poster, and he was arrested on the spot.

Billy Ray Waldon was tried, convicted and sentenced to death. He currently resides on death row at San Quentin State Prison.

Sarah Jane Whiteling

It was a hanging that outraged Philadelphians, the execution of a woman who claimed to have committed mass murder "in the interests of her children." The defense had offered an insanity argument, backed up by the accused's brother who testified that she had never been "quite right in the head." After the pronouncement of sentence, there had been petitions and letters to the editors of the city's daily newspapers. One of these had asserted that the execution of Sarah Jane Whiteling would "lessen the respect for women and womanhood." None of it did the condemned woman any good.

But how had it come to this? How had the matronly Mrs. Whiteling ended up in the dock and subsequently on the gallows? It started in early 1888, when Sarah Jane purchased a box of "Rough on Rats," a popular arsenic-based rodenticide of that era.

The Whitelings lived at No. 1227 Cadwallader Street, Philadelphia, at that time and were an apparently happy family. Husband John was a good provider and nine-year-old Bertha was growing to be a fine young lady. Willy, at age two, was the apple of his mother's eye. Then, in March of 1888, John Whiteling suddenly became ill and died within days in an agony of cramps and diarrhea. His death was ascribed to acute gastritis, and the doctor entered the same reason on the death certificates of Bertha, who died on April 25, and Willy who breathed his last on May 26.

But while the coroner might have been prepared to accept the verdict of "natural causes," Detective Frank Geyer of the Philadelphia police was not. Geyer, who would later achieve nationwide acclaim for his pursuit of the serial killer H.H. Holmes, did not believe in coincidences. Three unexplained deaths in the same family, all within the space of two months, sounded an alarm with him, and he was determined to get to the bottom of it.

Geyer's investigation soon turned up a possible motive for the murders. All three of the deceased had been insured. The amounts, admittedly, were small. But as a veteran detective, Geyer had seen men killed for less. He therefore set up an interview with the grieving Mrs. Whiteling and was unconvinced by her suggestion that her husband and children might have died after drinking contaminated water. If that were the case, why had she not become ill herself?

The detective's next step was to obtain exhumation orders on the three bodies, an exercise which produced exactly the result Geyer had expected. All three of the victims had consumed copious amounts of arsenic. Their bodies were riddled with the stuff.

Confronted with the evidence, Sarah Jane Whiteling soon confessed, now offering a different explanation for the murders. She said that her husband was a sickly man who had not been long for this world when she'd fed him arsenic to "ease his suffering." As for the children, she had known that she would not be able to support them without the help of their father. She had killed them, she said, so that they would never know "want or suffering." She had also intended killing herself, but her courage had failed her after the deaths of her loved ones.

Sarah Jane Whiteling went on trial in Philadelphia on Monday, November 26, 1888. Given the evidence against her, the defense was left with only one viable strategy – to plead her not guilty by reason of insanity. There was plenty of support for this, including the testimony of Dr. Alice Bennett of Northwestern Hospital. She testified that the defendant had "low mental organization" and was "undoubtedly insane." Two other experts, Dr. Charles Mills and Dr. John Chapin, backed up this opinion, while Mrs. Whiteling's own antics in the dock appeared to support their diagnosis.

In the end, though, the jury did not buy it. After listening to three days of testimony, they rejected the insanity defense and found Whiteling guilty of murder. The judge then sentenced her to hang.

Sarah Jane Whiteling died on the gallows at Moyamensing Prison on June 25, 1889. She is said to have gone eagerly to her death, telling warders that she was "going to join her family in heaven."

Robert Zani

Born in Tulsa, Oklahoma, on February 26, 1944, Robert Zani grew to be an intelligent child who got good grades at school. His parents had divorced soon after his birth, and Robert was raised by his mother, Gladys, with whom he had a close relationship. By the time Robert reached his teens, however, the bond between mother and son appeared strained. Zani would later claim that this was because his mother sexually abused him. Whether that is true or not, he continued to excel academically. In 1962, he enrolled at the University of Texas where he was a popular student.

Under the surface, though, all was not right with Zani. He was prone to periods of melancholy and to erratic behavior. He was also obsessed with guns and, in 1967, acquired his first firearm, a .357 Ruger Blackhawk. 1967 was also the year that Zani married Mexican national Irma Serrano Reyes, a former prostitute, and adopted her two children; it was also the year that he joined, and subsequently backed out of, the US Marines. And it was the year that he committed his first murder.

George Vizard was a contemporary of Zani's on the UT campus in Austin, although the two often clashed over political ideology. Vizard's political views were radical and socialist in nature, Zani's were decidedly right-wing. Yet the two of them worked part-time at the same convenience store, splitting shifts at Town & Country. That is, until Zani was fired in July 1967. A few days later, on July 27, someone walked into the store, marched George Vizard to the cold room, and shot him in the back. Zani, who was known to dislike Vizard, who probably had a beef over his firing, and who knew the layout of the store, wasn't even questioned by the police.

The next significant event in Robert Zani's life came in 1974, when his mother disappeared from her Tulsa home, never to be seen again. Robert, her only surviving relative, did not bother to report her missing. In fact, he continued cashing her Social Security checks right up until his arrest, several years later. In the meantime, he embarked upon a protracted crime spree, with his wife as an accomplice.

Zani's favorite targets were real estate agents. His well-worked M.O. involved posing as a prospective buyer wanting to view a property for sale. Once there, he'd draw a gun and rob the realtor of cash, jewelry, and credit cards, then leave the unfortunate victim tied up in the empty house. It was an efficient scam, but one that had the potential to turn deadly at any time. On April 4, 1979, it did. Realtor Julius Dess had been lured to an empty property in Corpus Christi, Texas, and robbed there at gunpoint. But Dess had panicked and tried to resist, and in the ensuing melee, Zani shot him to death. Dess was one of four victims believed to have died this way.

After the murder of Julius Dess, Zani fled with his family to Mexico, remaining there until March 1980 when he returned to Texas. That turned out to be a bad move on his part. On March 28, he and his wife, Irma, were arrested for credit card fraud, and Irma decided to cut a deal with prosecutors. She had some story to tell.

Not only did Irma Zani implicate her husband in the murders of George Vizard and Julius Dess, but she had an explanation for a six-year-old mystery, the fate of Gladys Zani. According to Irma, Robert had beaten his mother to death with a hammer, then dismembered her with a chainsaw before dispersing her body parts to various locations across Texas and Oklahoma.

Robert Zani was indicted for the murders of George Vizard, Julius Dess and Gladys Zani in mid-1980. After his conviction in the Vizard trial, resulting in a 99-year sentence, prosecutors decided not to go ahead with the Dess prosecution. In 1981, he was extradited to Oklahoma, to face second-degree murder charges for killing his mother. That earned him another 99-year term, although the conviction was later overturned on appeal. Zani is currently serving his time in Texas. He remains the prime suspect in three more murders.

For more True Crime books by Robert Keller please visit

http://bit.ly/kellerbooks

Manufactured by Amazon.ca
Bolton, ON

17534291R00120